Winning Lifetime Customers

Ho... ...sing Customer Care!

About the Author

Marc Thornton is a marketing consultant and trainer in Dublin, Ireland. He held senior marketing positions in AIB plc, Deloitte Haskins and Sells (now Deloitte and Touche), Securicor and Superquinn Supermarkets before joining DTA Marketing in 1994. He is now managing director of DTA Marketing. He works in Ireland and in Eastern/Central Europe including Russia, Slovenia, Slovakia, Czech Republic, Romania, Lebanon and Ukraine. Marc is a graduate and member of the Marketing Institute of Ireland.

Winning Lifetime Customers

How to *keep* Customers using Customer Care!

Marc Thornton

BLACKHALL
Publishing

This book was typeset by Gough Typesetting for

Blackhall Publishing,
8 Priory Hall, Stillorgan,
Co. Dublin,
Ireland.

and

Blackhall Publishing,
2025 Hyperion Avenue,
Los Angeles,
CA 90027,
USA.

Email: blackhall@eircom.net
Website: www.blackhallpublishing.com

A catalogue record for this book is available from the British Library

ISBN: 1 901657 67 1

Printed in Ireland by
ColourBooks Ltd

Contents

Dedication

Ann, Sarah and Debbie

Foreword

In today's business world the word 'change' is one of the most common buzzwords around. If we are to survive in today's and tomorrow's world we must change. Just take a quick look back over the last twenty years to see the dramatic changes that have occurred. These changes have not only occurred in the business world but across all life's activities. Our attitudes have changed and we have changed the way we do and see things. There used to be a saying that the only certain things were death and taxes. Maybe we should now add the word 'change' to this. In future we will not only be faced with change but with an ever-increasing pace of change.

With this ever-increasing pace of change our opportunity to retain lifelong customers becomes even more fleeting. After all, what is driving change is the consumer's need for faster, cheaper, better products. The choice for the consumer is wider and the ability to access their choice is now greater than ever before with the advances in technology. It is therefore essential that we look for and take on board new ideas on how we can retain customers. I have no doubt that Marc Thornton's book will become a valuable training tool in many companies.

I have known the Thornton family for over twenty years. Douglas and Frances, parents of author Marc, are two of the most hospitable people you would ever wish to meet. My first encounter with Douglas was in the West of Ireland in the early eighties when he was introducing innovative customer care programmes to Ryan Hotels. In those days, he was a pioneer in this area and many of the things he said and did are now commonplace. It was inevitable that Marc would inherit this same innovative spirit in the customer care area.

In this book Marc lays out his vision for winning lifetime customers in a clear and simple fashion. I found the book very easy to read with fine, real-life examples of the topic being discussed. It is one of those books where, as you read through it, you will ask yourself again and again, 'Why did I not think of that?' We all know that the simple message is the most effective and Marc's treatment of what can be a complicated issue makes the book easy to read and understand. There is a multitude of ideas that can be used by the smallest and largest companies in their customer retention programmes. It is not often that a book comes along which not only brings us back to basics but takes us forward with some innovative thinking as well.

I enjoyed reading Marc's book and it will certainly make essential reading for all my colleagues in the Company. If we could apply just a few of the ideas it would make a big difference to the way we do our business.

Pat McCann,
Chief Executive,
Jurys Doyle Hotel Group plc.

Introduction

I have been fascinated with marketing from the moment I started studying it in 1980. My first full time job in marketing was in 1982 and I have enjoyed every minute of it since.

Marketing activities are worthless unless every effort is made to keep customers. Many companies fail because they run out of first-time customers. Marketing and customer care are intrinsically linked. The fifth P of the marketing mix – people – has perhaps become the most important and most interesting part of the mix.

Customer care is not about a big WOW! It is about small things, little gestures and touches that make a difference when you are trying to delight the customer.

When writing this book I had several objectives in mind: make it practical and easy to read and understand; make suggestions on how to implement customer care rather than just talk about it; and share what I have learnt along the way so that you and I may get better service in the future.

Each chapter includes diagrams and charts, suggestions and checklists, and most importantly concludes by setting out key customer care strategies.

A workbook is included at the back of the book, chapters 9 and 10, which provides guidelines on how to implement marketing and customer care action plans. I hope they are useful.

For many years I have been giving seminars and training courses for educational establishments, institutes and companies. For those who attended those courses at last you will find a detailed version of the contents.

I hope you enjoy the book. If you have any comments or

suggestions please contact me at marc@dtamarketing.ie or visit our website, www.dtamarketing.ie, where you will find other interesting articles and further customer care ideas.

Acknowledgements

This book became a reality because of several people. My wife Ann had been saying for years that there was a good book in me. Tony Mason of Blackhall Publishing approached me with an idea about this book as a result of seeing articles by me in the *Sunday Business Post*, *Business Plus* and *Marketing* magazine. Thanks to Aileen O'Toole, Nick Mulcahy and Michael Cullen for giving me opportunities to have some of my ideas in print early on.

This book would not have been written without the inspiration and guidance of my father, Douglas. In the Thornton household, we were brought up on a diet of marketing principles and customer care concepts. It is no wonder that I followed Douglas into marketing — he has taught me so much and I am indebted to him for sharing with me (and others) his visions, practical solutions and immense experience over the years. My brothers, Paul and John, and my sister Nicola, all in the medical profession, are also utilising these marketing and customer care skills and they are making a difference in the way they do business and look after patients. Thanks Dad for everything. To my mother, Frances, a special word for all the encouragement, motivation, confidence and love over all the years.

I am very fortunate to have at Blackhall Publishing such a keen and dedicated team in Gerard O'Connor and Ruth Garvey. It was a pleasure working with you both.

Over the years, we have had many people work with us in DTA Marketing. They have all played a significant role in the company and some — especially Ali Toolan, Louise Lyons and Siobhán O'Reilly — have been of tremendous assistance with this book. I have learnt enormously from our clients and I would like to acknowledge their contribution also.

My friends and business colleagues have given me encouragement and practical advice, and have spent time editing and proofreading this text. A special thank you to Noel Jones who has amazing insight and a way with words, to Ian Brady, my friend and advisor for many years and to all the others too numerous to mention.

To my own family, a very special thank you. When we started on this journey (and it was one!) to write this book, we had no idea where it would take us. The many hours of researching and writing meant that I was not always there when I would have liked. Ann and our two beautiful daughters, Sarah and Debbie, have given me the space and time to write this book and I dedicate it to you. Thank you for your patience and understanding, your love and support.

Marc Thornton,
May 2001

Chapter One

Why Attract Lifetime Customers?

- Businesses are operating in a changing and challenging environment.

- It is marketing activities that attract potential customers.

- It is often the customer care they receive that keeps them.

- Some customers are more valuable than others — the challenge is to identify customers with the greatest long-term potential.

- Marketing activities focused on lifetime customers will be more rewarding and profitable.

- Key strategies — customer acquisition and customer retention.

Marketing activities attract customers but customer care actions keep customers.

We are living in a period of considerable change: everything and everybody is going faster, rushing and hardly stopping to think. Customers are becoming more fickle and taking advantage of bargains here and there — 'cherry picking' as retailers call it. It seems everyone is keen to get a bargain, from the less well off people, to those with plenty of cash to spare. Many conversations will include someone telling their friends of the deal or bargain they got on their house, car or stereo.

How can businesses hold onto customers if it appears that many customers just want the best price? Well, there are customers (short-term/casual) who just focus on price while other customers (loyal/lifetime) regard the after-sales service and continued support from the company to be crucial.

CHANGE

Suppliers to the consumer market have never had it so good according to Colin Gordan, Managing Director of C&C Ireland Ltd. In an article in *Marketing News* he observes that: 'In the Western World, consumers are living twice as long as their great grandparents; they are better off and more educated; they have better communications, more product information, more legal protection and higher quality of purchases than ever before'.

Companies have to be more innovative in order to gain a competitive edge in this new world and to attract new customers and to hold onto them. Companies such as Coca-Cola and Marlboro are moving into clothing where their brand name is acceptable. Superquinn Supermarkets together with TSB bank are opening Tusa Bank branches in their supermarkets. Retail outlets are open all weekends now, providing easier and longer access to their stores.

To get noticed in this highly competitive and changing market-place, companies are spending more on marketing and selling activities but also they are looking for innovative ways to attract and reach potential customers. The Internet with its e-commerce potential means shoppers don't have to leave home to shop. Supermarket shoppers can practically eat their supper in stores due to the array of sampling booths as they go down the aisle.

Products have shorter lifecycles than ever before due to increased competition and changing lifestyles. A few years ago every child wanted a Tamagachi (Japanese electronic pet) but where are they now? Products need to be robust — not just in the physical sense but also in the sense that they are constantly in demand by consumers. But even with all these product innovations, customers still need assurance on quality, service and the guarantee that they will be looked after if something goes wrong with the purchased product or service.

NEED TO DIFFERENTIATE

If a product or service is successful it will be copied quickly by competitors. The stage will be reached in a market where competing products or services are similar and prices can be changed and matched quite easily. There is often no superiority in availability as most customers can get the products or use the service where they wish. The challenge for marketers is to differentiate their product or service in the eyes of the consumer. For example, many companies are introducing longer opening hours, direct sales from manufacturer to consumer, loyalty cards, guarantees on price, improved service or increased customer care.

Federal Express — bar coding tracking

Customers can visit the Federal Express web page and, using a confidential code, can check where their parcel is while it is in transit. This use of Internet technology — 'extra net' — provides a competitive advantage as customers get a better service.

INCREASED COMPETITION

Most companies are facing increased competition from traditional as well as non-traditional competitors. With the opening of the European Union to increased internal competition, new entrants are appearing on the Irish market, such as the Bank of Scotland, offering lower interest rates on mortgages and forcing Irish companies to change their strategies. The Bank of Ireland was the first to react and matched the Bank of Scotland's lower interest rates and Tusa, the new TSB/Superquinn bank, has stated that it is offering the lowest mortgage rate in the country. Tusa has gained a competitive advantage over other banking institutions by introducing a six-function card that also logs points on Superquinn's customer loyalty scheme.

PROMOTE UNIQUENESS

Customers are looking for reasons to buy one product or service over another. With so many competing products and advertising, it is difficult for marketers to get their message across. Marketers aim to communicate the unique selling points (USPs) of their products or services to the target audience.

The uniqueness could be on price. For example, DID

Dell Computers — direct model

Michael Dell, as a college freshman in 1983 at the University of Texas, began buying excess computer parts from retailers to make and upgrade PCs. Reselling these improved systems was a great success. In his first full month of business he sold $180,000 worth of computers. Dell, like Bill Gates, never showed up for his second year of college.

By the end of its first financial year as a public company (Michael Dell was only 23 years of age), Dell Computers recorded sales of $257.8 million. The strategy was to sell direct. Companies and consumers could decide from the catalogue and order PCs over the telephone. Because it dealt directly with its customers, Dell could also foresee what its customers wanted. In the process it developed a reputation as the sophisticated buyers' computer company — its machines weren't the cheapest on the market but they were highly regarded for being the latest and best at reasonable rates. Dell has turned to the world wide web to sell its products directly to consumers and small businesses. The company now sells more than $5 million a day on the web.

By accessing www.dell.com you can order your computer to your own specification and the price will be calculated onscreen. Payment is followed by prompt delivery and supported by an extensive team of experts on the telephone from their European support centre in Bray, Ireland.

Mr Topler, Vice-Chairman has said: 'Dell will sell what its customers desire'.

electrical shops promote a 'double the difference' message where they will refund customers twice the price difference between one of their products and a competitor's, if the competitor's is cheaper. Another unique approach is to focus on the product features or benefits. Rolls Royce in its famous advertisement written by David Ogilvy stated that 'at 60 miles per hour the loudest noise in the new Rolls Royce comes from the clock'.

The key to promoting and selling products or services is that the targeted customers notice the difference, like the difference and want to buy.

BEHAVIOURAL CHANGE

Consumers' wants and needs are changing and it is the responsibility of marketers to interpret what is required at the present time and to predict their future needs. For example, people travel abroad more than ever before. Ryanair, Ireland's independent airline, offers the most economic flights to Europe and its expansion reflects the demand for travel. Belfast International Airport was the tenth most profitable company in Northern Ireland in 1998.

The Internet has opened our eyes to a vast network of knowledge and information. *Encyclopaedia Britannica* is now available free on the web and you can search for any topic among its 300,000 web pages. The only catch is that there is advertising on most pages which funds the cost of all this free information. You can also pay for this virtual encyclopaedia and view it without the advertisements!

Disposable income is rising as more households have two salaries. Consumers are looking for increased value as well as durable and high quality products. Excellent customer service is demanded as time has become more precious and consumers want everything now!

EMPLOYEE SKILLS

More is expected of staff these days. Staff must be knowledgeable about the products or services, be customer oriented and have the skills to sell profitably. Companies have to spend more on training than ever before to ensure that their staff are prepared for the demands of customers. Yet in certain industry sectors there are considerable difficulties in attracting and keeping staff especially the entertainment and leisure sectors. Staff retention is a key issue and will be explored later in this book.

Universities and institutes have seen the impact of demand on businesses and are changing the contents of courses to meet the needs of students and professionals and their future marketplace. The Institute of Certified Public Accountants in Ireland (CPA) has introduced Market Place Strategy (marketing) on its Professional 1 course.

CUSTOMER VALUE AND LOYALTY

Businesses are becoming more selective. They don't want *every* consumer — they want the higher-value customers which they can look after and keep for many years. Maintaining customer loyalty is becoming a key strategy for businesses today. Once you have acquired a customer the challenge is to keep that customer satisfied and loyal to your company.

> Companies spend five times more on customer acquisition than on customer retention.

In a general sense a customer can be divided into three categories according to their profitability:

1. Those who generate profits	20%
2. Those on whom the company breaks even	60%
3. Those on whom the company loses money	20%
	Customers

This indicates that some customers are subsidising others. A number of questions need to be asked following this analysis:

1. Are we attracting the right type of customer?
2. Is our focus on the wrong end of the market or is it too broad?
3. Should our marketing resources be centred on particular segments that have long-term potential?
4. Can we convert non-profitable customers into profitable customers?

How a company responds to these questions/reviews will determine their future profitability.

> Lifetime customers are those customers whose needs a company can keep on satisfying and whose profit potential justifies the effort to retain them.

Lifetime customers are loyal, give referrals and are likely to be quite profitable. Marketing programmes should focus on attracting customers with the best lifetime potential. Marketers do this by analysing their marketplace and identifying lifetime customer types. A lifetime customer is likely to stay with an organisation for at least ten years.

Companies also need occasional or once-off customers to achieve short-term sales targets. The pressure to achieve quarterly results to satisfy shareholders expectations means that senior executives must focus on immediate results (short-

---

Profiling profitable customers

Analyse:
- size of the customer and volume of purchases
- longevity of the customer relationship
- purchasing patterns such as timing, frequency and average purchase size
- product mix purchased
- pricing realised
- cost to acquire
- cost to serve
- a customer's potential for generating referrals.

Source: Cambridge Management Consulting

---

term profits). Marketing activities need to attract instant buyers as well as give messages that demonstrate the company's commitment to the concept of a lifetime relationship.

Buying customers

An organisation must learn to think of itself not as producing goods or services but as buying customers, doing the thing that will make people want to do business with it.

Source: Theodore Levitt 'Marketing Myopia' *Harvard Business Review* (1960)

LIFETIME CUSTOMERS MEAN LONG-TERM PROFITS

Do you know how much a lifetime customer is worth to your business? The answer could startle you as it is probably higher than you imagined. If a customer buys all their cars from you or uses you as an insurance broker for all their insurance and pension needs, how much would they spend with your company over a lifetime? A conservative estimate at today's prices would be:

- car purchase ∈170,000 (11 cars in lifetime)
- insurance broker ∈400,000 (pension, life assurance, home insurance).

A lifetime may, for some, appear a very long time. If you regard a lifetime in terms of customer loyalty as ten years only, the figures are still quite considerable. Take a regular shopping trolley at a supermarket (average ∈100 a week for a modest sized family) and calculate the spending over ten years. This comes out at ∈50,000!

Using the same method, the following values apply to other industry sectors over ten years:

- petrol (∈30.00 a week) = ∈15,000
- pub/restaurant (∈80.00 a week) = ∈40,000.

Only a modest investment is required to keep customers (e.g. customer care training, customer satisfaction surveys etc.) as compared to the cost (marketing and selling) of attracting new customers. Existing and loyal customers are quite profitable. That is why many leading companies are investing in keeping their customers after having gone to the expense of attracting them there in the first place.

Keeping a customer for life can only be achieved if we succeed in making the customer feel really special and valued and looked after by us. If, however, we are successful in doing this, then something even more valuable to our business occurs – this customer will recommend us to other people. Suppose our customer recommends us to two or three new customers and they in turn are treated in the same way as we treated our first customer. What might happen next? In their turn, our new referred customer could become a lifetime customer and go on to recommend us to two or three more and so on. The value of lifetime customers keeps on increasing as more referrals are made. The following example shows this.

Calculating the value of lifetime customers

Year 1
If a customer uses our petrol station and shop each week and spends ∈30 for 50 weeks a year, this will total ∈1,500. If the customer is really *delighted* they may become a regular *lifetime* customer and spend ∈1,500 a year for 10 years. This amounts to ∈15,000.

Year 2
If this customer recommends us to three other people who become customers, and if we are successful in *delighting* them and they become *lifetime* customers (10 years), their value will be ∈45,000.

Year 3
The three customers from year two could each recommend three more people who could be worth up to ∈135,000.
And so on — as long as we keep on *delighting* all our customers.

Customer retention is a combination of selecting, training, motivating and setting high standards of customer care. The 18-year-old motorbiker enquiring about insurance at an insurance broker could, if looked after very well spend, over ∈40,000 on motor insurance premiums with that company over the next 40–50 years. If that person making the enquiry felt special and important because of the way the staff looked after him or her, there would be no reason to change insurance broker in their lifetime.

Sometimes we don't take customer queries seriously. A depositor leaving a telephone message for their bank manager may not get a reply for a few days. The depositor may have invested elsewhere in the meantime and all future savings and pensions will also go there because the banker didn't bother to respond quickly.

Getting noticed and talked about by customers among friends and family is one of the primary objectives of the lifetime customer strategy. When people hear of the positive endorsements by their friends of a particular company's products or services, they don't need to read too much more information about it — they just go and purchase.

Concept of lifetime customers

The concept of looking at customers from a long-term or lifetime viewpoint may change the way companies treat customers. Companies are inclined to view each individual transaction as a 'once-off' exercise. The concept of a lifetime customer requires companies to view the customer on a long-term basis and not just as another customer here to bother staff.

There are considerable benefits of attracting and keeping lifetime customers. Customers do not normally change where they buy unless the service is bad or they have a difficult or bad experience.

Benefits of lifetime customers

- stay for 10–20 years
- tell other potential customers about the product or service
- profit potential increases over time
- good, long-lasting personal relationships are developed.

Customers can be converted into lifetime customers if they are well looked after or are delighted with the product or service. Unfortunately we do not know which customers will become lifetime customers and which ones will use us for a single transaction. So we must treat *all* customers as though they are lifetime customers and perhaps they *will* become lifetime customers!

Conclusion

When a new customer buys a drink at the bar, fills the car with petrol or buys a loaf of bread, it could be their first visit to your establishment. Here is a fantastic opportunity to demonstrate that you offer more than other pubs, cafés, petrol stations or shops.

Unfortunately many staff regard new customers as strangers and prefer to focus on the regular customers as they are easier to talk to and deal with. As a result, staff lose this golden opportunity to impress and convert the stranger into a lifetime customer. Staff need to look beyond the initial value of the transaction and see the full potential of the relationship in the long term (i.e. see the lifetime customer). They may then treat the stranger differently. The following points are therefore important to bear in mind:

1. We do not know which customers will evolve into lifetime customers so we must treat all customers as though they will become lifetime customers (perhaps they will!).
2. Customers who use only one product of a company's portfolio may need more products or services in the future — this provides sales opportunities.
3. Delighted customers will refer other customers and perhaps reduce the need for some future marketing activities and save on expenditure.

4. The cost of replacing a lifetime customer is very expensive as the income forgone is not just this customer but all the possible referrals that will be lost to your competitor!

> So we must treat *all* customers as though they are lifetime customers and perhaps they *will* become lifetime customers!

Chapter Two

Attracting and Keeping Lifetime Customers

- Marketing and customer care are intrinsically linked.

- Marketing messages should support the concept of lifetime relationships.

- Marketing programmes should focus on attracting customers with the best lifetime potential.

- Difficult to share price and customer care messages.

- Short-term and longer-term marketing messages are different.

Man without smiling face should not open shop.

Chinese proverb

Most businesses need to attract and keep customers in order to survive. It is very rare for a business to open for trade with customers beating a path to its door! Even if a business is phenomenally successful in its early days, it cannot assume this demand will continue and needs to implement marketing and customer care activities to ensure its continued success.

It is marketing activities that attract potential customers to a business. When a potential customer makes contact, the selling then takes place. Superior customer care is then needed to keep the customer. Marketing and customer care are intrinsically linked if a company is serious about its long-term future.

Customers have a huge choice. They can buy elsewhere and often do. Many companies don't even realise when a customer has left — they just don't seem to be around as much or they buy less. Sometimes staff are too busy to even notice, in some cases staff don't care as they have thousands of other customers!

The concept of looking at customers from a long-term or

lifetime viewpoint may change the way companies go about attracting and keeping their customers. As we saw in Chapter 1, some customers are worth more than others; some have significant potential while others will rarely purchase more than one item.

The challenge is to find the customers with enough sales potential and to devise marketing and customer care programmes to attract and keep them. However, in order for a business to survive it will probably be necessary to attract, in the short-term, customers who may not be repeat customers. These different customers will probably need different marketing messages and activities.

It is important to realise that you cannot know which customers will become lifetime customers and which ones will use you for a single transaction. If we treat a stranger as though they are a once-off customer — then they will be! If we regard each customer as a potential lifetime customer — then it is more likely that they *will* become one.

You must treat all customers as though they are lifetime customers.

MARKETING AND CUSTOMER CARE

Marketing

Marketing is about identifying and anticipating customer needs and wants and matching them with products or services at a profit.

Customer care

Customer care is about looking after customers so well that they stay loyal and buy more and also tell other potential customers about the attention and service they received.

What it is	**What it is not**
• a positive helpful attitude to customers	• flavour of the month
• anticipating customer needs	• charm school ethics or false smiles
• resolving complaints quickly	• words with no action
• getting everyone to focus on keeping customers	• insincerity or lip service
• delighting customers.	• something that will bring instant results.

Marketing and customer care are intrinsically linked. However, the importance of one over the other will vary depending upon the relationship. Marketing activities are used to attract potential customers and convert enquiries into purchases. Customer care will keep customers and ensure they remain loyal and repeat purchase.

In order to attract lifetime customers we need significant marketing activities but also, very importantly, we need an element of customer care. Lifetime customers want to be reassured that the company is focused on giving good value, will respond to their concerns or complaints and show that it cares that the customer is pleased with the product or service that is purchased. In order to maintain an existing customer, some marketing and promotion is needed but mostly it will be superior customer care that will keep them.

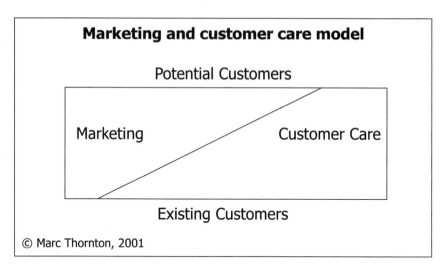

Marketing messages that include customer care/service messages will have a lasting impact. Superquinn uses the slogan 'more for your money!' which implies a focus on service and quality.

A company's reputation for customer care will enhance its prospect of attracting lifetime customers. It is likely that the advertising messages will confirm what is already thought about the company. If little is known about the company, then it is imperative that the correct message is communicated. There is also a higher probability of attracting lifetime customers if the marketing message supports the concept of lifetime relationships.

Lifetime customers

The profit potential of a lifetime customer increases over time as good, long-lasting personal relationships are developed. Lifetime customers are likely to stay for 10/20 years and most importantly, will tell other potential customer about your products and services.

Existing customers have heard the message, purchased the products or services and now are likely to need good customer care if they are going to be repeat customers. For example, hotels are focused on attracting new customers all the time. However, once the customer has arrived the focus switches to customer care and every effort is made to ensure that they enjoy their stay and leave as delighted customers.

To attract customers there is more focus on marketing activities with some focus on the customer care message, while keeping customers is primarily focused on customer care activities with some reinforcement of the marketing message.

The value of customers

Murray Raphael quotes a customer taking advantage of a special offer at a travel agency who had difficulty with a disinterested staff member because of the extra paperwork required. He eventually reminded the travel agent: 'You are an overhead, I am profit'.

TARGETING POTENTIAL CUSTOMERS

Marketing programmes should focus on attracting customers with the best lifetime potential. It makes sense to target the more valuable customers from a future potential point of view. For some supermarkets, e.g. Tesco, Dunnes etc. families will represent significant future sales while for others, e.g. Marks and Spencer, single occupancy households or apartments will buy most of the convenience or 'ready to cook' range that they prepare and sell.

Each company should review its customer base and identify the characteristics of its customers that have the most potential. The marketing messages should focus on this sector. The reason the major Irish banks — Allied Irish Bank and Bank of Ireland — battle it out for the franchise to locate their student branches in the main universities is because of the significant future potential when these students become business managers and professionals. Students each autumn are offered an array of gifts if they open an account with the bank. It is well known that most customers of banks do not change to another bank unless the service is deplorable or, of course, if their loan application has been turned down!

'Under-marketing'

There is a danger of 'under-marketing' — leaving it too late to try to attract the high potential customers. For instance, by the time a student is qualified and working it may be too late to encourage them to open a bank account. In the case of travel agents the age group of 50–60 years is very attractive as they are the individuals who are spending more time on travel. This includes holidays and in the case of many, visiting their grown up children who live abroad. They don't decide on a travel agent at 55 years of age — they already use one! Therefore, a significant part of the marketing budget should be spent on attracting pre 50–60 year olds.

Short-term and long-term marketing

Nearly every company needs sales in the short term to survive. The main marketing activities commonly used include price cutting, sales promotions, incentives, loyalty schemes and increased advertising. In many cases this conveys an image of a company that focuses on the product or service rather than the customer care side where price is the most important feature.

> An industry is a customer satisfying process, not a goods producing process — it is vital for all business people to understand this.
>
> *Source*: Theodore Levitt, 'Marketing Myopia' *Harvard Business Review* (1960)

In Eastern Europe, companies that advertise aggressively and intensely are often perceived to be desperate for sales and conversely potential customers often don't buy.

Advertising and communication messages that focus on price normally exclude the other aspects of the business, e.g. guarantees, delivery, technical support etc. There simply isn't enough room to communicate other messages when the focus is on price. These types of advertisements need to send clear messages in order to get an immediate response, e.g. 'three for the price of two' (lemonade), '25 per cent extra free' (shaving foam), 'buy now pay later' (computers), ∈19.99 per week (new cars), 'was ∈29.99 now ∈19.99' (kitchen cooking pots).

What kind of customers are attracted utilising price-focused advertising and sales promotions? Price-focused customers! These are customers who will change brands for lower prices. They are not focused on the services offered with products and do not appreciate customer service. They are therefore probably not the type of customer you would expect to purchase from you in the long term. In fact they won't because they will go elsewhere since they are focusing on price alone.

However, focusing on price alone would suggest that a company is not too concerned about repeat purchases. Some companies fail to realise the damage that can be done to the brand in the long term because of their short-term focus on price. It is very rare that you can put your prices up (except inflation equally increases). So how you project your image is vital from the very beginning. Price can be an important part of that message but not the only message.

Reduced prices if explained sensibly can be increased or

reverted to normal (regular price) when the special promotion/ event is over. In this way the brand attributes (e.g. quality, back up service, customer service) can be maintained in the longer term.

It is very difficult and costly to maintain the low price or free offers beyond the initial period. Many companies have run into difficulties on this. Some companies have got a reputation for frequent sales so if you want to buy a significant product from them now, it is advisable to wait for the next sale as it will nearly always appear every six to eight weeks.

It is difficult to change the message from price focus to quality and customer care focus in the short term. Customers can easily get confused. If Microsoft sell some software at a very cheap price and others at quite an expensive price they will confuse their customers. It would be perceived that some software is not good and is sold very cheaply and in other cases (i.e. expensive prices) that the customer is being overcharged.

No free lunch

AltaVista withdraws its free Internet access, start-up ZapMe reneges on its free services and PCs for schools, and online convenience store Kozmo adds a delivery charge to its services.

Short-term marketing doesn't mean ignoring pricing in its message. It is how it is conveyed that is important. Customers want value for money and value is much more than low prices — recognition of price is important in a company's message. Some companies fail to promote price completely, e.g. small opticians rarely make price offers while their competitors, the large retail outlets (multiples), are always promoting 'two pairs of glasses for the price of one'. When customers see no attempt to convey price attractiveness, they are likely to assume that the prices are expensive which is not always the case.

Superquinn are perceived to be quite expensive even though price surveys show that on comparable products, e.g. dry goods/groceries, their prices are similar to their main competitors. This perception comes from the quality image they convey, their high reputation for customer service and perhaps because they make or stock lovely fresh food that is so tempting to buy! For many years Superquinn used the slogan 'come for the prices and stay for the service'. Price signage can clearly be seen in all the Superquinn stores which is constantly communicating to the customers that price is important and is part of the value proposition at Superquinn. When asked how many sales staff work in Superquinn by the chairman of WalMart, a leading supermarket chain in the USA, Senator Feargal Quinn proudly said: '365,000 — our customers'.

While recognising that companies need sales at all times (in the short and long term) it is prudent to take the long-term marketing viewpoint in planning communication with target audiences. How a company positions itself will have a lasting image with potential and existing customers. Getting it wrong at the beginning could prove to be costly later on. It is difficult to change from a cheap, low quality image to a more expensive product range with the focus on superior customer care.

CONCLUSION

Customers form an opinion of products or services that is vital to the future long-term growth of the company. Selecting the type of customers and sectors you wish to focus on is very important. Decide on the profile of the customers with significant lifetime potential and devise a positioning strategy that will ensure consistency in your communication and recognition by the target audience of the intended messages.

All marketing and customer care activities need to be part of an overall marketing plan. Marketing plans are discussed in more detail in the Workbook at the back of the book.

Consistency in the messaging and positioning is crucial if we want to convert potential customers into purchasers. Since most advertising is missed or not observed by people, it is likely that an advertisement must be seen between four and seven times in order for it to be noticed. Potential customers must see and understand the message.

In the long term, the focus must be on customer loyalty. Companies must identify what its high potential customers need and ensure they deliver it.

Price, as the old saying goes, is long forgotten after the purchase is made. Customer service will often become a key differentiator for customers as they search for value and expect companies to look after them. This can be seen in the case of repairs, warranty and when changing items even though they had been purchased some time ago.

Key customer care strategies

- Treat all customers as though they are lifetime customers.
- Marketing and customer care activities should be planned for potential as well as existing customers.
- Include marketing and customer care messages in customer communication in order to position the company and its products as a customer-focused organisation.

Chapter Three

Customer Loyalty

- Customer loyalty/satisfaction model describes four categories of customer.

- Different strategies and actions are required for the different categories of customer.

- How to convert 'trapped' and 'promiscuous' customers into 'lifetime' customers.

- Action plans are needed to implement customer care.

Loyal customers are made not born!

The aim of most businesses is to attract and keep lifetime customers. Delighted customers will be very loyal and very satisfied. However, you can also have customers who are very loyal but are quite dissatisfied! They feel trapped as they probably have no option about moving to another company (e.g. utilities — power, water).

Likewise you can have very satisfied customers but they need your product on an infrequent basis. They will, however, be excellent ambassadors for your company, as they will tell friends about the quality product or service they received. They could be described as 'sleepers' as they await the occasion to repeat purchase. When they need to repurchase they will have no hesitation in purchasing from your company again.

There are nevertheless customers who are not loyal to any company or product/service and are prepared to move for lower prices, sales promotions or incentives. It is likely that they are briefly satisfied by the price but are likely to be dissatisfied later as the quality may not last and low priced products or service are not usually accompanied by good customer service.

These aspects are often forgotten while the purchase is being made. I call these types of customers 'promiscuous' as they are not very loyal and frequently change brands. I have devised a customer loyalty/satisfaction model to explain this concept (see overleaf).

'Lifetime'

Lifetime customers will purchase regularly, tell their friends and show appreciation to staff. In order to attract and retain this type of customer they must notice the difference in your product offering and/or the level of customer service provided. This is explained later in the book when delighting the customer is discussed.

Customer loyalty/satisfaction model

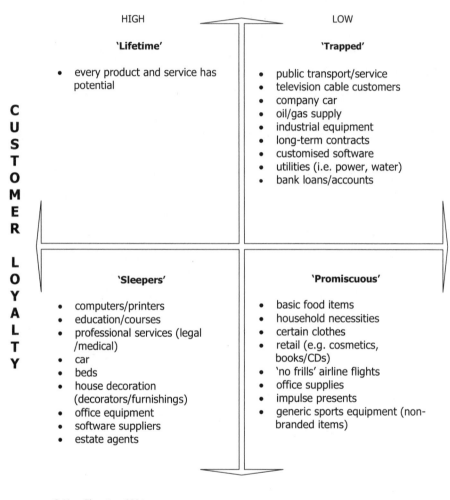

CUSTOMER SATISFACTION

HIGH ⟶ LOW

'Lifetime'

- every product and service has potential

'Trapped'

- public transport/service
- television cable customers
- company car
- oil/gas supply
- industrial equipment
- long-term contracts
- customised software
- utilities (i.e. power, water)
- bank loans/accounts

'Sleepers'

- computers/printers
- education/courses
- professional services (legal /medical)
- car
- beds
- house decoration (decorators/furnishings)
- office equipment
- software suppliers
- estate agents

'Promiscuous'

- basic food items
- household necessities
- certain clothes
- retail (e.g. cosmetics, books/CDs)
- 'no frills' airline flights
- office supplies
- impulse presents
- generic sports equipment (non-branded items)

CUSTOMER LOYALTY

© Marc Thornton, 2001

'Sleepers'

The customers who we call 'sleepers' purchase irregularly but are very loyal when they do. They have significant potential and should be maintained on the database. They should also be included in mail shots/newsletters so they are updated on product developments and customer service improvements.

'Trapped'

The customers who feel trapped and who have no choice are very dangerous to a company. They will spread negative word of mouth. It is important that companies listen to their concerns and act accordingly. Due to the imminent deregulation of many monopolistic markets (thanks to the European Union), many companies, especially state companies, will be facing competitors for the first time. Then customers will have the opportunity to vote with their feet!

'Promiscuous'

The customers we describe as 'promiscuous' are ones that are easily persuaded to change. They do not appreciate the finer aspects of the service as they don't want to pay for them. They may view the product purely on its merit/usability and therefore do not wish to pay more for the quality aspect or the expected customer service. For instance, Ryanair, the low fares airline company, doesn't offer anything extra — just the flight — and you pay for drinks and food. That company is also unlikely to pay your hotel accommodation if there are delays causing you to stay at the airport overnight — a 'no frills' package as they say.

The strategy is to convert all customers into lifetime customers. This is where superior customer care and marketing activities can have a significant input.

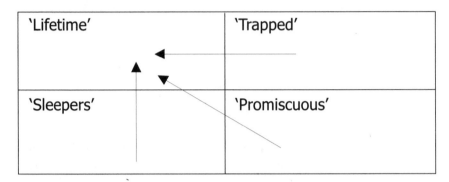

'Sleepers'

It is important to keep in touch with the customers we call 'sleepers'. They need to be aware of new product offerings, improvements in customer care and in particular they need to know that their custom or business has been appreciated.

While special and exclusive offers are quite valuable, 'sleeper' customers do appreciate you asking their opinion and looking for their suggestions. It is also a subtle way of keeping in touch and telling them about recent developments.

The following chart describes their position and suggests actions and strategies that can be utilised for the different categories.

Customer loyalty/satisfaction model

CUSTOMER SATISFACTION

HIGH	LOW

'Lifetime'

Description
- repeat purchase regularly
- tell friends
- will complain, get treated well and stay
- appreciate staff (tips and thank you letters)
- may have heard through positive word of mouth

Actions
- need specific advertising (show USPs to attract them)
- they must *notice* the difference
- deal with complaints quickly and '+1'

'Trapped'

Description
- cost of switching is high
- have 'no choice' or to change is costly
- recognise better products/services elsewhere but can not change due to contract
- will spread negative word of mouth
- don't believe they are getting good value for money

Actions
- listen and respond to complaints
- demonstrate customer care improvements
- act like your customers could leave
- show your appreciation for their custom
- ask their opinion on how to improve customer care training

C U S T O M E R   L O Y A L T Y

'Sleepers'

Description
- infrequent needs
- recommend to friends but may not need to repurchase themselves
- high potential to spend in the future
- needs have changed (i.e. new job/older children)
- single purchaser rather than company or family (modest needs)
- circumstances change (i.e. move /change job)

Actions
- keep in touch
- maintain on database
- inform about new products/services
- research their needs
- thank them for their custom

'Promiscuous'

Description
- price conscious
- not loyal/easily persuaded to change
- don't appreciate customer service (e.g. after sales support)
- favour own label (lower price)
- quality not a high factor in their decision
- satisfied primarily on price

Actions
- indicate customer care aspect
- send mixed messages (price and quality)
- improve the customer service
- compete on price but highlight service aspects

© Marc Thornton 2001

'Trapped'

Customers that feel trapped do appreciate your efforts to improve the service. Again market research can be very valuable — it shows you care even if the service is not perfect. It is important to demonstrate that the company cares and values their opinion. Efforts to improve the customer service will be noticed and will make them feel less trapped.

One should use every opportunity to demonstrate the good value they receive whenever possible. Training in customer care is very important as friendly, trained and customer focused staff can reassure customers if the service is unsatisfactory and this in turn discourages them from spreading negative word of mouth.

'Promiscuous'

While it is very important that the price message is part of the promotion, other benefits and customer care aspects should be highlighted also, e.g. our expert staff, same day delivery, money back guarantee if not satisfied etc. Providing free information (e.g. leaflets) and educating your customers (e.g. cooking instructions) will take their focus away from the price aspect alone. They will appreciate that there is more to a product or service than price.

CONCLUSION

If the aim is to convert casual customers (or strangers) into lifetime customers then a plan is needed. Customer care is an important part of the marketing mix and must be included in the marketing plan. Remember: lifetime customers are made not born!

An appropriate action plan for customer care can be

developed after considerable thought and analysis of the marketplace, company goals, customer needs and marketing programmes. The following chapter sets out how a marketing plan can be written.

Key customer care strategies

- Analyse the customer loyalty/satisfaction model to plot where your customers are presently located.
- Aim to convert 'sleepers', 'trapped' and 'promiscuous' customers into 'lifetime' customers.

Chapter Four

Plugging the 'Leaky Bucket'

- Listen to customers — find out why they leave.

- Implement listening systems.

- Utilise market research technique to gather constructive suggestions.

- Devise customer care action plans to eliminate leaks.

Shoppers decide in the first eight seconds when visiting a retail outlet whether they are comfortable and therefore likely to buy.

Most businesses carry out some marketing activities throughout the whole year to attract more customers. Yet, if they could hold on to their existing customers, they would not have to keep spending large amounts of money on marketing. What many companies don't realise is that while they are constantly gaining new customers, at the same time they are losing customers.

Chris Daffy (1996) in his book *Once a Customer, Always a Customer* describes this phenomenon as the 'marketing bucket'. I suggest that it is called the 'leaky bucket' as you can visualise a bucket being filled from the top with new customers and at the same time losing customers out of the holes in the bottom.

WHY DO CUSTOMERS LEAVE?

The main reason why customers leave is because of indifferent staff. Customers who were researched say that they found the staff to be rude and unhelpful. It is not that members of staff intend to be uncooperative; it may just appear that way to customers. Customers hear the words 'can't' or 'won't' or 'we are unable' and they get the impression that staff are being unfriendly. Sometimes it is the systems or operations procedures that limit what staff can do. These restrictions hamper staff in the delivery of the service. For instance, in a certain restaurant in Temple Bar, Dublin, the chef is not allowed to serve sole 'off the bone' or deviate from the menu. I know because I have eaten there — once!

Why do customers leave 'leaks'?

- 68 per cent leave because of indifferent staff who just don't care
- 10 per cent are chronic complainers
- 9 per cent find somewhere cheaper
- 5 per cent move on recommendation
- 4 per cent are natural floaters
- 3 per cent move away
- 1 per cent die.

Source: Chris Daffy, *Once a Customer, Always a Customer* (Dublin: Oak Tree Press) 1996

This research indicates that members of staff have a key role to play in keeping customers. The way they communicate and interact with customers is vital so staff selection, training and motivation are critical to a company's success.

There is a constant need to use marketing activities to attract new customers because, for a variety of reasons, we keep losing customers or some just don't return.

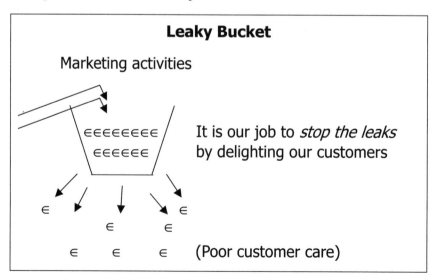

Leaky Bucket

Marketing activities

It is our job to *stop the leaks* by delighting our customers

(Poor customer care)

Murray Raphael, the direct marketing guru, says that the average business loses 20 per cent of its customers every year. A study in the *Harvard Business Review* by Frederick F Reichheld and W Earl Sasser Jr entitled 'Zero Defections' stated: 'if you could keep just 5 per cent of the customers who leave ... you could nearly double your bottom-line profit'. Since it is well known that it costs five times more to attract a new customer compared to keeping a customer, there is a constant need to analyse why customers leave.

The following are examples of why customers leave:

- There was nothing special about the way we were treated (i.e. not a memorable experience).
- Members of staff were rude and unhelpful (indifferent).
- Operational issues (e.g. late deliveries, wrong products delivered etc.).
- Product issues (e.g. product characteristics didn't match promise).
- Service issues (e.g. opening hours unfriendly, company not contactable during lunchtime or evening, no back-up if staff member not available, unable or unwilling to repair products, slow service, automated transactions with no contact with staff).

> 65 per cent to 85 per cent of customers who leave say they were satisfied with their former supplier.

First impressions

Shoppers decide in the first eight seconds when visiting a retail outlet whether they are comfortable and therefore likely to buy.

THE FIVE Ps (PRODUCT, PRICE, PLACE, PROMOTION AND PEOPLE)

Marketing activities are intrinsically linked with customer care. The marketing mix, which is summarised by Philip Kotler's four Ps — product, price, place (distribution) and promotion — help attract customers to the company's products/services. But it is recognised that it is the customer care activities carried out by staff (the newest P! — people) that hold onto customers. So the 'leaky bucket' theory could be described as a combination of the five Ps of marketing. The four Ps are used to attract customers and the fifth P (people) is used in the form of customer care to keep customers!

In the marketing of services, some writers have described the marketing mix as the seven Ps. The additions being process, physical evidence and people.

When we have gone to the trouble of attracting customers we need to make sure we pay them attention and don't give them any reason to leave.

Many staff members believe it is the employer or boss who pays the wages. They may authorise it, but the money comes from the customers. Staff members need to be made aware that it is income from customers that allows the boss to pay the salaries. So every customer is valuable and members of staff have a vested interest in keeping customers.

Customers pay the salaries!

Eleanor Deveney of Henkle Ecolab sent me the following note (it can also be found on many websites). It illustrates very well how many companies miss the point when they have eventually attracted the customer into their promise.

Remember me?

I'm the person who goes into a restaurant, sits down patiently and waits while the waiter or waitress does everything but take my order.

I'm the fellow who goes into a store and stands quietly while the counter staff finish their little chit-chat.

I'm the man who drives into a service station and never blows his horn, but waits patiently while the attendant finishes reading his book.

Yes, you might say I'm a good guy. But do you know who else I am?

I'm the fellow who never comes back, and it amuses me to see you spending thousands of pounds every year to get me back when I was there in the first place ...

And all you had to do was show me a little courtesy!

HOW TO FIX THE 'LEAKS'

'If only we knew what was causing the leaks we could stop customers leaving'. This is a common expression you hear from exasperated entrepreneurs and business owners. So how can we learn what is causing these 'leaks'?

Market research, while formal in its methodology, can be quite comprehensive but it doesn't substitute for mixing with or listening to customers directly. Bill Gates, founder of Microsoft, spends 25 per cent of his time with customers. Senator Feargal Quinn of Superquinn can often be seen packing bags on the shop floor. Their aim is to listen to customers and find out at an early stage if there are any problems that could lead to customer 'leaks'.

So we need to develop listening systems. Listening is the key. If you are not willing to listen to customers, it is likely you will go out of business. Customers' needs keep changing and if a company does not constantly change to meet their new needs then your customers will go elsewhere.

An analysis of recent surveys indicates that on average 80 per cent of customers are 'satisfied' or regard the products or services as ordinary. This is dangerous as satisfied customers are only temporarily loyal and can easily move on if some better offer or product is available. It is important to find out how your customers rate your company.

A poor rating will focus management and staff on making improvements. A positive rating will reinforce the customers' positive orientation of the company and motivate staff to keep up the good work and not get complacent.

Key listening systems include:
- comment cards
- questionnaires
- customer satisfaction surveys
- focus groups
- mystery shoppers
- observation.

Comment cards

Comment cards are short questionnaires (5–8 questions) that can be left on your premises (e.g. shop, hotel) for customers to complete or can be sent out for postal reply. Most hotels, restaurants, retail outlets and other service industries are now increasingly using this method of getting customer feedback (e.g. Powerscourt Golf Club asks members and visitors to complete comment cards at their club). You can expect compliments but most importantly you are likely to get negative comments which in fact you will find very useful.

Case Study — Powerscourt Springs Health Farm

Powerscourt Springs is Ireland's premier luxurious health farm and for very good reasons too. Guests are invited to complete a short customer comment card on leaving. They are asked to rate the services and facilities on a scale so that over time improvement or disimprovements will be noted. The directors are keen to learn what customers think about the health farm and to gather any suggestions they might have. Guests often make very constructive suggestions and many are implemented immediately.

The responses are collated so that each month there is an overall rating and a monthly moving average.

Each section of the health farm is measured and every guest's comments are included in a weekly report for the management meeting. Instant responses are made to dissatisfactions and interesting complementary comments are noted for advertisements and PR material.

Powerscourt Springs is so successful that a weekend break must be booked several weeks in advance.

The weekly report is put on the staff notice boards so that all staff can see the comments whether complimentary, constructive or negative.

Tips for designing comment card

- keep it short, i.e. 5–8 questions
- include rating questions
- name/address should be optional to get back replies
- ask for the type of product/service purchased
- always provide an opportunity for comments using the phrase 'any other comment' (leave space for remarks)
- explain purpose of seeking their comments
- encourage criticism
- thank customers for providing comments.

It is very important to test questions on a few customers before you go to print!

Questionnaires

Questionnaires are the most common form of market research as they can be used for:

1. Postal surveys.
2. Telephone surveys.
3. Personal interviews (e.g. on the street).
4. In-depth interviews (face to face).

The sequence and design of questionnaires is crucial to the success of the research project. I always use the 'funnel approach' (see diagram overleaf). This makes it simpler to design the questions and also easier for the customer to complete. The early general questions will prepare the responder for the more crucial and key questions later on. They will have thought about the subject and are more likely to give an informed answer to the key questions.

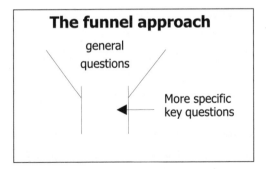

The number of questions can vary depending on the type of survey. Only a few questions can be asked if the survey involves stopping people in the street as they will normally be in a hurry. Many questions can be asked if it is an in-depth interview in the person's own home.

Tips for designing questionnaires

- explain the purpose and thank customers for completing it

- have general questions at the beginning with more specific questions later on (funnel approach)

- for awkward/personal questions use options/ranges rather than specific or direct questions, e.g. age — Under 20 ☐ 20–30 ☐   31–40 ☐ etc.

- make it fun/enjoyable to fill in, e.g. ☹ ☺ ☺ (please tick)

- if giving a prompted list of possible answers include:

  Other ☐ Please specify _____

- always explain ratings, e.g. 10 = excellent, 1 = very poor etc.

- ask several questions together, e.g. 'Please rate our staff out of ten (10= excellent, 1= very poor) for:
  Product Knowledge ☐ Appearance ☐ Helpfulness ☐ etc.

Unfortunately the response rate to questionnaires is extremely low, even if a company surveys its own customers. It is generally regarded that a response rate of 2–5 per cent is the norm as customers/respondents often feel that there is nothing in it for them. There are always exceptions of course but considerable effort is required to increase the response rate.

Some surveys have got spectacularly good response rates, e.g. 40–50 per cent while others get negligible results. Here are some ideas that have worked for me:

- make it short: 1–2 pages
- enclose a stamped self-addressed envelope
- encourage a fax reply and design the questionnaire so the respondent just has to put it in a fax machine as your fax number is at the top already
- encourage a reply with free gifts, prizes or the promise of headline results
- provide a good explanation of why you want them to complete it and how you will improve the products/services with their comments and ideas.

Customer satisfaction surveys

Customer satisfaction surveys are becoming more and more popular these days as businesses want to benchmark their performance with customers. By benchmarking (knowing where you stand at this moment in time) your company's performance as well as changes in customer perception can be measured over time and you can find out what activities have worked and which ones weren't even noticed.

Customer perception is their reality.

It is important that companies do something with their results. It is too easy to dismiss and ignore poor results with a flippant remark. You will often hear: 'they don't know what they're talking about' or 'they are obviously misinterpreting what we are trying to do'. For a customer, what they see and think is very real and this can affect their purchasing.

Bank of Ireland — customer surveys

Bank of Ireland, one of Ireland's leading financial institutions, has been carrying out customer satisfaction surveys for many years now. Three times a year each branch and business unit is surveyed.

In addition to an overall satisfaction rating, customers are asked to assess each aspect of the service. This survey was, until recently, sent in the post to randomly selected customers for a postal reply. It is now being carried out on the telephone in order to speed up the response rate.

An interesting outcome from this is that the results are discussed at the branch manager's annual review, as the aim is to increase the overall satisfaction ratings of their customers as well as the performance of the branch.

Different styles of question to get the best results

(a) Ask customers to rate several topics in one question

Please rate your answers out of 10.
(10=excellent, 1=very poor)

Your staff

Product knowledge ☐
Appearance ☐
Helpfulness ☐
Friendliness ☐

The service

Speed of service ☐
Accuracy ☐
Choice/range ☐

(b) Provide a wide choice

Indicate where in the range (circle number) you would
rate the following:

Staff:
Very helpful 10, 9, 8, 7, 6, 5, 4, 3, 2, 1 unhelpful

Staff:
Knowledgeable 10, 9, 8, 7, 6, 5, 4, 3, 2, 1 not knowledgeable

(c) Use boxes

Tick box (out of five). Indicate which word describes the
correct answer:

Excellent   Good   Average   Poor   Very Poor
☐   ☐   ☐   ☐   ☐

(d) Introduce some fun questions/symbols where possible

Describe our service:

Great service   Average service   Poor service
☺   ☺   ☹

(e) Ask open questions for deeper understanding

'Why do you drink Guinness?'

_____

_____

Focus groups

Focus groups are informal group discussions with customers or potential customers conducted by an experienced researcher to examine aspects of the product or service in greater depth. They are invaluable in gathering information in a subtle way from your most valuable critics — your customers.

These informal discussions can be attended both by non-customers and customers. Superquinn Supermarkets conduct a customer focus group every week. Therefore, they have 40 a year and these are personally chaired by Senator Feargal Quinn, chief executive of Superquinn.

These groups provide great feedback to senior executives and store managers on what is causing the 'leaks' or reasons why customers are dissatisfied, or don't wish to return. In addition, if the chief executives are involved, they get an incredible insight into the minds of their customers and can therefore make more customer-oriented decisions.

During these discussion groups it is advisable to always look out for the 'lone dissenting voice'. Constructive criticism is vital and should be encouraged. Bias must be avoided and the facilitator must have an open mind as to the outcome of the discussion.

Below are a number of ideas for planning and running focus groups:

1. Select different types of customer (segment your customer base and ensure all relevant sectors are represented).
2. Choose a convenient time for your target audience (e.g. morning for housewives etc.).
3. Devise an agenda so that all aspects that need discussion are covered.
4. Choose an appropriate order for the sequence of the discussion (e.g. general topics then become more specific, visualise travelling around the retail outlet and comment on each area in turn).

5. Make sure the surroundings, environment etc. are appropriate (e.g. comfortable chairs) and create a friendly atmosphere to encourage participants to be open and honest.
6. Invite criticism — good and bad news is needed.
7. Don't be defensive — ask and decline to comment yourself until the end.
8. Don't have more than two executives at the session. Instead, suggest the session is recorded and others can hear it later.

Mystery shoppers

Mystery shoppers are great! They tell it as it is. If you really want to find out why customers leave and don't return, get an experienced customer or a professional mystery shopper research service to visit your outlet and, using an agreed approach, provide feedback on their experience.

You will be amazed what you will find out. This is a test of how members of staff behave towards customers when senior personnel are not present. Advance Pitstop, Ireland's leading tyre and exhaust suppliers and fitters, carry out mystery shopper surveys so that they can improve the service they provide. They even record the 'customer' telephoning the outlet and asking for prices. Playing back the tapes to the staff can be fun! But there is a serious purpose to this exercise as the aim is to have all outlets providing the same high quality of service.

Some retail outlets carry out mystery shopper competitions among the outlets in their group, which can produce extraordinary results. The following case study on Sweeney Oil, a leading West of Ireland retail and wholesale petrol group, explains how a mystery shopper competition really works.

Case Study — Sweeney Oil

Sweeney Oil has a 'station of the month' competition using mystery shoppers. As enlightened and visionary owner John Sweeney himself says: 'We want our customers to be delighted that they have chosen one of our petrol stations. If we treated all our customers as though they were the judges of our mystery shopper competition then we will certainly improve the service we provide.'

In a six-month period Sweeney Oil has carried out customer care training with all staff, introduced staff motivation and staff retention schemes and launched a 'station of the month' competition.

The aspects of the service and expected customer care behaviour were clearly set out. Each station received feedback from the mystery shoppers in the form of marks and comments and particular members of staff were mentioned if their customer care behaviour was exceptional.

One of the petrol stations increased its petrol volume by 30 per cent in that six-month period. It's no coincidence that this particular station won the first 'station of the month' award and it also won the petrol distributor award for the best volume increase in its area.

Powerscourt Springs Health Farm also uses 'mystery shoppers' to order brochures and book a programme and treatments. Then reports are sent out to the directors. These unbiased reports are very valuable for planning further training and ensuring agreed standards are being met on a consistent basis.

The following points should prove useful when planning a mystery shopper campaign:

- Agree the criteria to be measured with managers and staff.
- Select experienced impartial people or specialists to make visits.
- Run a competition in conjunction with the visits.
- Have more than one visit as everyone can have one bad day!
- Share and evaluate the results with all staff.
- Owners and managers need to buy into the concept and believe the results.
- The emphasis of reports should be on customer care systems with careful and constructive comment on the staff.

Observation or 'shop floor' research

Top customer care companies carry out informal 'shop floor' market research. This involves executives of a company mixing, in a casual way, with customers and potential customers as they consider purchasing your product.

Senator Feargal Quinn of Superquinn does not pack bags or work the checkouts because they are short of staff! No, he wants to hear from customers about their shopping experience and what in particular they disliked about the service provided. He wants to fix those customer care 'leaks' by hearing directly from the customers themselves.

Marketing managers and advertisers of top brands are regularly seen in supermarkets beside their product display as they chat informally to customers about the packaging, advertisement and usefulness of instructions that are on the packs.

Hotel managers spend most of their day on the 'shop floor'. Charlie Costelloe, general manager of the 4 Star Plaza Hotel in Tallaght, Dublin regularly asks diners in the hotel's Olive Tree restaurant if they are enjoying their meal. He doesn't ask: 'Is everything ok?' or 'Is everything alright?' as most restaurant managers do. This is a question that focuses on us and how we are performing. He wants them to think about the food and the service that they are receiving so he asks them: 'Are you *enjoying* your meal?' (which is about them) and in this way he can find out if there are any potential 'leaks'!

DEVISING AN ACTION PLAN

Now that the causes of these 'leaks' have been found, it is imperative that they are eliminated. A customer care action plan is needed to set out what needs to be done, by whom and by what date. Suggestions for the structure of an action plan will be provided later on in the book.

CONCLUSION

In order to find out about those 'leaks':
- encourage constructive comments and complaints
- put in a listening system
- ensure results are discussed at management meetings
- ask customers where or how the service can be improved
- ask non-returning customers why they left (utilise your database to track them).

In my experience I believe that the following reasons are regularly the cause of 'leaks':
- poorly trained and indifferent staff
- badly planned systems which affect customers
- poor products or services
- no clear complaints policy
- poor focus on customer care.

Key customer care strategies

- Listen to customers on a regular basis.
- Encourage constructive comments and complaints.
- Find out the causes of 'leaks'.
- Devise an action programme to eliminate 'leaks'.

Chapter Five

Using Customer Care to Delight and Keep Customers

- Always aim to *delight* the customer.

- Dissatisfied customers can be turned into delighted customers.

- Staff get recognition and appreciation for anticipating customer needs.

- Use of customer's name can enhance friendliness of service.

- Analysis of the 'moments of truth' resulting in an action plan will improve the service provided to customers.

Delighting customers is not more of the same — it is about providing something different and better than your competitors!

Having attracted customers to your business it is vital that you now make every effort to keep them. What are companies doing to keep customers returning? Below are some examples:

1. Portraying a friendlier image. For instance, using their name when answering the telephone, e.g. 'Good morning Jones Business Systems, Elaine speaking'.
2. Thanking customers for their business, introducing loyalty schemes, e.g. Superclub from Superquinn or the Value Club Card from Dunnes Stores.
3. Keeping in touch with customers, even occasional purchasers. For instance, Farrelly Dawe White, accountants and registered auditors in Dundalk and Dublin, send quarterly newsletters to all clients and contacts on their database to keep them informed of tax changes and to remind them of deadlines for tax returns etc.
4. Follow-up calls to ensure customers were pleased with the service. For example, the banqueting section of each Jurys Doyle Hotel will ring conference bookers the next day after the event to get instant feedback.

Here are some facts about customer care:

1. Companies spend five times more on customer acquisition than on retention.
2. Most companies don't hear from 96 per cent of their dissatisfied customers as very few complain, they just don't return.
3. Dissatisfied customers tell 20/30 people about their bad experience.
4. Satisfied customers tell no one — they don't even notice.

5. Delighted customers are six times more likely to repurchase than satisfied customers.
6. Delighted customers tell 7/10 other people so 'word of mouth' will attract more customers.

CUSTOMER EXPECTATIONS

I'm sure you will agree that customers expect more now than ever before. Even as customers ourselves when we go to a restaurant or pub we expect quick service, good choice of food, friendly staff and good value for money. If anything is not up to the standard we expected, we are likely to leave and not return. We probably won't even complain, although I think we are becoming less tolerant and do complain more than before.

Customers have greater choice than ever and are not willing to accept sub-standard products or services. They have become more educated and expect higher standards of customer care through their experiences and the provision of superior service by leading customer-orientated companies.

General customer expectations include:
- appropriate speed of service
- good value
- fast and satisfactory response to problems or complaints
- friendly and pleasant staff
- competitive prices
- availability (hours of opening)
- quick response to queries and requests
- quality products or service.

It is very important to set standards in customer care and then to measure how your company performs. The methods of finding the 'leaks' outlined in Chapter 4 are also useful for the measurement of existing customer care standards.

> If you are not happy with anything you have bought from us, we will give you your money back.
>
> *Source*: Sign in café at Vienna Airport.

For instance, British Airways found that late departures caused all sorts of problems for customers so they came up with a customer-oriented initiative (see page 64).

Understanding the power of customer care

Many companies have realised that providing superior customer care will enhance company profits. Many customer care problems stem from having inexperienced staff serving customers. Therefore, staff training can be effectively utilised by all companies — small and large.

> Compared to marketing activities, customer care is inexpensive and in many cases more effective!

To learn how customer care can be a profitable activity for your company, it is necessary to understand a few basic customer care concepts.

Aiming to delight the customers

> Delighting customers is not more of the same — it is about providing something different and better than your competitors!

There are three types of customers:

1. Dissatisfied.
2. Satisfied.
3. Delighted.

Case Study — British Airways

Reducing late departures by eliminating late arrivals

Four new initiatives to speed your journey

1. Gates now closing ten minutes before take-off:

Please note that from 1 February 1999 we are closing our gates ten minutes before departure. That means everyone gets seated, we take off and you arrive on time. If you are running late and reach the gate within ten minutes of take-off, we can't guarantee you'll be allowed to board — in which case, we'll book you on the next available flight.

2. Weigh hand luggage at check-in:

We're now weighing hand luggage at check-in to prevent delays when you are boarding.

3. New boarding card:

You'll notice we've introduced a new boarding card with clearer boarding and departure information.

4. And if you're working:

You can now carry your laptop as hand luggage on any of our aircraft — and that's in addition to your normal cabin allowance.

Please also remember our minimum check-in times. They mean we can all get away on time.

Source: leaflet sent to British Airways loyalty card holders

It is not enough to satisfy customers, they need to be 'delighted' according to Tom Peters the well-known management writer. He and Philip Kotler are responsible for introducing the word 'delight' into customer care thinking. And they are right!

Delighted customers are six times more likely to repurchase than satisfied customers.

When you buy your morning paper and get the correct change, it would be fair to say you were satisfied. How many people did you tell about this purchase? None I bet — though you were satisfied.

> Satisfied customers tell no one!

Recently I had my car serviced. Not only did I get a replacement car for the day but my car was washed and vacuumed. I was delighted and told many of my friends. It was not a big 'wow' but it was different and better when compared to other garages. Some services are not visible or tangible so you can make an impression by doing something extra and visible, like a cobbler who could polish your shoes for free after making the repairs.

> Only 21% of satisfied customers said they would
> 'definitely' return and purchase.
>
> *Source*: *Marketing News*

Research in the USA tells us that dissatisfied customers tell eleven of their friends about a bad experience. My own research in Ireland indicated that Irish people, if dissatisfied with a product or service, will tell between twenty and thirty people. Negative comments by customers (or former customers) can be devastating for business.

> Dissatisfied customers tell 20/30 others!

On the other hand, delighted customers tell their friends about the experience — perhaps seven to ten other people will hear about it.

> Delighted customers tell 7/10 others!

Delighting the customer

When Saturday evening diners at Dublin's Unicorn Restaurant leave to go home, they are presented with a complementary copy of *The Sunday Tribune* so that the memory of great food and friendly service at dinner is extended over the weekend with this customer care thought.

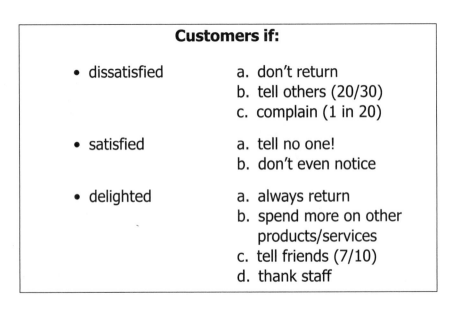

Customers if:

- dissatisfied
  - a. don't return
  - b. tell others (20/30)
  - c. complain (1 in 20)

- satisfied
  - a. tell no one!
  - b. don't even notice

- delighted
  - a. always return
  - b. spend more on other products/services
  - c. tell friends (7/10)
  - d. thank staff

So how do we delight the customer? Sometimes it is innovative thinking or new ideas. On some occasions, customers tell us how to delight them if we are listening. They may not use those words exactly but they may say 'why don't you ... ?' and make a practical suggestion. If members of staff are good at listening they will pick up these good ideas. Also we can simply copy what others are doing and modify and improve on it for our industry and our company.

Delighting the customer is not just about doing one thing exceptionally well — a big 'wow'. It helps of course! However, delighting customers is about doing small things for customers, on a regular basis, that were not expected but certainly liked. Therefore, activities that delight customers must be noticed and liked.

Customers must notice the difference and like it.

Aim to:

- deliver exceptional customer care =>increased profit
- spend less on advertising and more on converting occasional customers into lifetime customers.

Amongst other things, customers have been 'delighted' when:
- their name is used at the checkout till
- their wipers and headlamps are cleaned at a petrol station
- their shoes are polished when left in for repairs
- restaurant managers ask: 'Are you enjoying your meal?'

It is difficult work for staff to focus on delighting customers all the time but it is very rewarding. For staff working in the service sector where customers 'tip' exceptional performance, considerable extra income can be earned. In other areas it can be very satisfying to observe customers thanking staff and showing their appreciation. They also buy more and return on a regular basis and tell their friends. This leads to retention of your existing customers and growth of your business when they tell their friends. So delighted customers are very profitable.

To delight a customer we should be sure to give them our *full attention*. This means:

1. Eye contact.
2. Observation.
3. Anticipation.

Eye contact

Watch out for customers coming into your outlet. Eye contact with customers or browsers is very important as it shows our interest in them and with a nod or a wave we can indicate that they will have our assistance in a few moments.

Lack of eye contact can show considerable disinterest or no appreciation. Look at bar staff when the bar is very busy. They rarely make eye contact with customers, which causes considerable unease if you are trying to get their attention, even if you want to find out that they will be serving you soon.

At the checkouts in supermarkets and retail shops, it is very pleasant if the cashier makes eye contact and thanks you for your custom. It shows that your custom is appreciated.

Observation

Members of staff who are alert and interested in delighting the customer will observe their actions and respond accordingly. How many times have you tried to find items in your local store and searched the shelves without any staff member responding? Wouldn't it have been marvelous if a staff member saw you looking for something and immediately came over to you and asked: 'Can I help you find something?' I think you would return to that shop again and perhaps describe the staff to your friends as 'friendly or helpful'.

Members of staff need to become skilled at observing customers and take the initiative to offer assistance. Inspirational leaders, such as Senator Feargal Quinn of Superquinn, are often seen helping customers on the shop floor. Senior managers and owners should lead by example. Staff should be acknowledged for their initiative so that they will be encouraged to increase their observations of customers and improve the service.

Anticipation

Staff should try to learn how to anticipate customers needs. They will get credit from customers for anticipating or asking if a customer wants something. If a customer asks for something they will expect the staff to respond and no credit and little appreciation is given. A petrol station might anticipate their customer needs and plan the following:

1. Always have a plentiful supply of soapy water and sponges for cleaning car windows.
2. The shop should have plenty of baskets to carry the shopping in.
3. Always check that the most popular items are in stock.
4. Offer to carry bags to the car.

APPROACH TO CUSTOMERS

Are you treating strangers or first time customers the same as lifetime customers?

If you know a person is going to spend ∈ 50,000 with your company over the next ten years, will you go out of your way to ensure they are well looked after and get special treatment? Of course you will.

Murray Raphael is so convinced of this lifetime customer concept that he suggests companies give the first order free as this customer is going to be so valuable to the company over the coming years. A challenging thought!

Use of customer's name

Imagine a stranger walks into your petrol station and has ∈50,000 printed on his forehead to indicate his future value to your company. Do you jump? Yes, of course you do! Yet it regularly happens that when a stranger or occasional customer buys petrol using a cheque book, credit card or petrol club card, their name is not mentioned. It is as though they are just another transaction and the staff doesn't care.

Using a customer's name will make a considerable difference. The trouble is we don't know if this stranger will become a lifetime customer. So we must act as though they might and you never know, maybe they will. Many companies adopt a policy of deliberately focusing on the stranger. In this way any visitor will be very well treated. Casual and regular customers will see how all potential customers are treated and it will probably confirm to themselves that they have chosen well.

The following is a list of ten basic needs of customers everywhere:

1. They need to feel *welcome*.
2. They need to feel *comfortable*.
3. They need to be *understood*.
4. They need *assistance*.
5. They need to feel *important*.

6. They need to be *recognised.*
7. They need to be treated with *respect.*
8. They need to be *listened to.*
9. They need *prompt service.*
10. They need to *trust* you.

Examine the list and observe that using a customer's name will respond to any of these basic needs. Some petrol stations use the name on customer cheques and credit cards to personalise the transaction, e.g. 'have a safe journey Mr Brady' or 'nice to see you again Suzanne'.

I estimate that seven or eight of the above needs of customers of retail outlets will be partially met if their name is used. Members of staff need to become focused on getting and using customers' names.

With advances in technology, especially e-mail and the web, customers can receive personalised messages from the company which will make them more noticeable than their competition, e.g. the general manager of a hotel can e-mail recent guests thanking them for staying at the hotel nearly before they arrive home.

Unique selling points (USPs)

Each company should examine why it attracts customers. What are your unique selling points (USPs)? This should be the basis of an interesting analysis. Don't forget to tell your customers why you are special. If you cannot find anything unique or special about why customers come to you, they may not continue to purchase from you.

Some companies have been quite innovative in devising and promoting their USPs. For instance, the Ryan Hotel Group have 'friendly fellows' to entertain the children while parents can relax and enjoy their holidays (and get a few moments of peace!). The concept of the 'friendly fellow' was devised by my father, Douglas Thornton and the chief executive of the Ryan Hotel Group, Conor Mc Carthy, in the early 1980s when Ryans decided to focus on family holidays. Many Irish families have been entertained by 'friendly fellows', including my sister Nicola and brother John, over the years and had memorable holidays. It has made a noticeable difference as repeat customers account for most of Ryan Hotels' customers.

Another example is that of an insurance broker who recently expanded her opening hours and now her firm is the only broker open during lunch in a midland town.

Dr Paul Gueret opens his Baggot Street medical practice in Dublin at 7.00 a.m. so that patients not wishing to miss work can visit their doctor or have insurance medicals carried out at times that suit them. These longer and earlier opening hours will facilitate patients getting an appointment more promptly.

I suggest you ask your colleagues to complete a short list of the USPs of your company. Having agreed this list you should then look at your marketing material, advertisements brochures and letters, and make sure that all these USPs are included.

My guess is that in most cases some of these USPs are not set out in a clear and concise way for potential customers to see. Are your USPs clearly set out in your company material and are they a key feature of your marketing messages? If they are not it is obvious then that they are 'secrets' and you are wasting valuable opportunities to impress potential customers.

Make sure there are no 'secrets' otherwise you may be losing customers or not taking advantage of cross-selling opportunities.

Don't keep your USPs a secret.

Case Study — Skoda

Improved customer satisfaction means more sales!

Skoda has been ranked the number one manufacturer for customer service in the 1998 JD Power / *Top Gear* survey. It is the first time that Skoda has taken number one position and it is also the first time a European car maker has taken the top place, which in the past has been the stronghold of the Japanese.

The customer satisfaction survey of 29,000 recently registered cars, carried out in conjunction with the BBC's renowned *Top Gear* programme and magazine, and the market research group, JD Power, revealed that Skoda was top of all car manufacturers (34 in total) in the provision of exceptional levels of customer satisfaction. The survey researched into three areas of customer satisfaction:

1. Problem incidence/resolution.

2. Vehicle performance.

3. Customer support.

Skoda scored the highest in two out of three categories and improved its performance over last year's results in every area, outperforming the world's automotive giants.

From fifth position in 1997 Skoda has outperformed all other manufacturers by taking number one place as the leader in customer satisfaction. The rejuvenated Skoda brand, now part of Volkswagen/Audi Group, has shown continuous improvement over the last three years and is one of only three brands to have shown improvement every year (the other brands are BMW and SEAT which also belongs to the Volkswagen/Audi Group).

Not only has Skoda improved its performance in customer satisfaction but in 1997 it recorded its best ever sales' success in its UK history: 16,500 customers bought into the Skoda brand, an increase of 24 per cent on 1996.

According to Colin Sheridan, sales manager for Skoda in Ireland, an extremely high proportion of Skoda owners have registered satisfaction with their cars, with 85 per cent of owners confirming that they will purchase another Skoda next time round.

Source: Press release from Skoda Ireland

ANALYSING THE 'MOMENTS OF TRUTH'

A customer forms an impression about a company based on how well the company performs at the 'moments of truth'. These 'moments of truth' are all the occasions that a customer is in contact with an organisation. On the basis of that contact, the customer forms an opinion about your product or service and its quality.

The 'moments of truth' can be illustrated utilising a diagram called the 'Cycle of Service' model. This model shows all the 'moments of truth' for a customer while visiting a bar or restaurant. In this case there are ten 'moments of truth'.

The challenge for companies is to take each moment and analyse their performance at this point of interaction with customers. Many companies set customer care standards for how the staff behave on these occasions. The setting and implementing of customer care standards will be discussed in the next chapter.

When Scandinavian Airlines Systems (SAS) were performing below expectations in the late 1980s, the then CEO Jan Carlzon assessed the performance of the company to ascertain where it was performing well and where it needed improvement. He came up with this concept of the 'moments of truth' and he and his colleagues set about improving all these points of contact that they had with the customer.

So your customers will assess your company from the moment they contact you by telephone or letter to the welcome and service at the counter, the sale, even the way you thank them for their business.

There are many types of 'moments of truth' of which six are the most critical. These are listed below.

Cycle of Service
Showing ten 'moments of truth'
Example — bar/restaurant

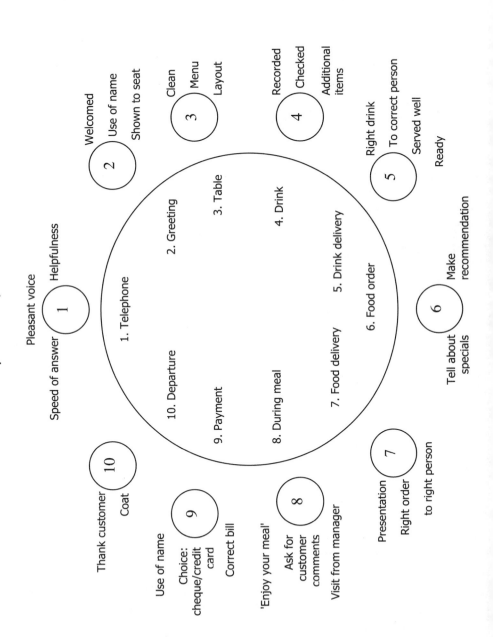

1. Telephone
 - Speed of answer
 - Pleasant voice
 - Helpfulness

2. Greeting
 - Welcomed
 - Use of name
 - Shown to seat

3. Table
 - Clean
 - Menu
 - Layout

4. Drink
 - Recorded
 - Checked
 - Additional items

5. Drink delivery
 - Right drink
 - To correct person
 - Served well
 - Ready

6. Food order
 - Tell about specials
 - Make recommendation

7. Food delivery
 - Presentation
 - Right order to right person

8. During meal
 - 'Enjoy your meal'
 - Ask for customer comments
 - Visit from manager

9. Payment
 - Choice: cheque/credit card
 - Correct bill

10. Departure
 - Use of name
 - Thank customer
 - Coat

The six critical 'moments of truth'

1. Buy/no-buy:
   The moment of truth when the customer decides to actually buy your product/service — or not.

2. Value for money:
   The moment of truth when the customer assesses the value of the product or service — this could be some time after the initial purchase.

3. Repurchase:
   The moment of truth when the customer decides that 'I will buy this again'.

4. Referral:
   The moment of truth when the customer decides to recommend your product or service to other potential customers.

5. Bad news:
   The moment of truth when the customer finds out how you really react when your business systems fail. Can you still deal with the customer?

6. Perpetually recurring:
   These moments of truth occur every day and you may not be around to manage them. For example, starting the car or turning on the TV. Each of these is a moment of truth for the customer.

Source: Karl Albrecht and Lawrence J Bradford, *The Service Advantage*, 1990

You might like to analyse your company's contact with your customers. It might bring up some interesting points for discussion.

For instance:

1. Payment: we accept cash, cheques and visa but not Amex or Access. Why not?
2. Telephone: no one to answer the telephone during lunch. Do we have an answer-machine? Why not?
3. Packaging: look at the ways products are packaged when leaving the store — the quality of the bags; are boxes offered?

Companies and staff should analyse each of these 'moments of truth' and objectively assess if they are performing well. If there is room for improvement then the staff ideas and customer comments should be taken on board and acted upon.

The intention should be to anticipate customer needs and then offer something extra. This is a great way of using the 'moments of truth' to help delight the customers.

WELCOMING THE STRANGER

Have you ever walked into a shop and the members of staff were too busy talking to a colleague, a friend or a regular shopper to even notice you. In this case you could be the stranger but what the shop assistants don't know is how much you might spend today or over the next five to ten years if you liked the store, its products and the service.

Murray Raphael categorises customers utilising a concept he calls the 'loyalty ladder'. When a browser or 'tyre kicker', as they are called in the motor trade, goes into a shop, they are often regarded as a nuisance as they are not purchasing today. However, browsers will sometimes become occasional customers. If they are very pleased with the product and service they might return. Often it is only when they become regular customers that staff take serious notice of them.

The loyalty ladder

← Advocates
← Regular Customers
← Occasional Customers
← Browsers/Suspects

Delighted customers will tell others. Murray Raphael calls them advocates as they will proactively tell others about the service they experienced. Since we don't know if a browser will become a regular customer we should welcome browsers (or strangers) and they may become a customer in time.

Key Customer Care Strategy:
Welcome the stranger!

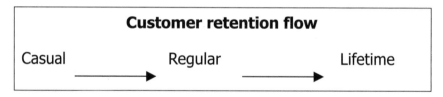

Customer retention flow

Casual   Regular   Lifetime

Louis Copeland, Ireland's best-known tailor and men's outfitter, while being interviewed on the radio was asked what was his favourite book. He mentioned Murray Raphael's (1995) book *Up the Loyalty Ladder* as having a profound influence on his approach to business and if you ever visit any one of Louis Copeland's outlets you will know why, as he and his staff 'walk the talk', i.e. put this concept of treating browsers as lifetimes customers into action.

CUSTOMER CARE PROBLEMS MADE PUBLIC

If customer care problems become public it can have serious consequences for staff morale and future sales.

A leading personal computer manufacturer, whose core business is selling direct to the public, has admitted that it has been having problems with its technical support operation. The problem was that customers had been left holding for incredibly long periods of time on the telephone waiting for assistance. It would appear that the technical support section was seriously understaffed.

Negative customer care issues if made public, as this example was in the *Sunday Business Post*, will discourage future buyers and will certainly reduce repeat purchase even if the poor customer service was not experienced directly. The increase in expectations by customers for better service has encouraged more customers to contact radio talk shows like Marian Finucane, Joe Duffy or Pat Kenny on RTÉ Radio One or write letters to the editor of *The Irish Times*.

Poor service completely takes away the good value one received at the time of purchasing the product. Customer service is an integral part of a product. It is very difficult to recover from negative publicity in the area of customer care, even if a company rebuts the press story. Many existing and potential customers will not see the correction or retraction in the next day's newspapers. Many companies would also find it difficult or inappropriate to announce a few days later that the problem had been rectified. The story correcting the mistake may make more people aware of the original problem and therefore compound the problem.

One strategy to deal with negative publicity is to admit the mistakes, inform the media how the problem is going to be rectified and encourage customers to try the service again in a short while.

Dealing with complaints

Dealing with complaints gives staff an ideal opportunity to respond to a dissatisfied customer. If a complaint is properly handled, a dissatisfied customer can be turned into a delighted customer. Staff must learn from complaints. Companies actually need complaints in order to learn how to improve the service.

Key Customer Care Strategy:
Encourage complaints!

Here in DTA Marketing we have devised a special complaints handling policy to make sure that no customers go away dissatisfied. In fact, you can turn a dissatisfied customer into a delighted customer by following this policy. So if a customer complains:

1. Thank them for bringing it to your attention.
2. Apologise and say that you are sorry they are upset (whatever is the cause of the complaint). It is important that you say you are sorry that they are *upset* rather than saying you are sorry that, for example, 'there is no car wash today'.
3. Immediately offer to fix the problem and offer something else or have the problem looked after.
4. Fix it at no cost to the customer.
5. Be generous and do *something extra*.

Encouraging complaints

We should encourage complaints because:
- only 1 in 20 complain
- we need to learn from our mistakes
- it is an ideal occasion to make an impression.

Fixing complaints quickly

The biggest disappointment for most customers is how they are treated when they have a complaint. In fact, the reason so few customers complain is because their experiences have so often been disappointing. They no longer complain, they just don't come back and they tell their friends instead of complaining.

Why customers do not complain

- staff not interested in complaint
- nothing happens after complaining
- might get staff into trouble
- staff might prove the customer to be wrong
- customers don't want the hassle.

There are many benefits to be gained from fixing complaints quickly.

Advantages of fixing complaints quickly

- improves relationship with customers
- enhances reputation
- reduces costs
- keeps customers
- attracts customers due to positive word of mouth.

Customers have a better relationship and trust with a company if they know that their problems/complaints will be resolved quickly and in a friendly manner. It can become very expensive for a company if complaints remain unresolved. Other customers will hear about it and the customer might leave for a competitor. The actual cost of fixing the complaint will increase with time delays. The customer is likely to get more upset and contact senior people in the company to get the problem resolved and they may have to be generous by way of compensation to get the situation corrected.

We need to respond to complaints quickly, as the longer it takes to fix a complaint the more expensive it gets. That is why we must pay attention to the 1/10/100 rule, which I came across when reading about a leading international hotel group.

1:10:100 Rule – fix complaints quickly

Let's take the following example of an unsatisfactory hotel meal to illustrate the rule:

If we fix up a complaint (for example the beef might be tough) as soon as we hear about it, it will cost the company (raw material – more beef) a small amount say €1.00. If the complaint is fixed at a later stage, for example at the reception desk in a hotel as a guest is leaving, the drinks and wine bill may be removed from the bill at a cost of €10.00 perhaps. If the complaint remains unresolved or not resolved to the satisfaction of the guest after they have left reception, they may write to the managing director pointing out the failure of staff to settle the issue. The managing director will have to give generous acknowledgement of the unresolved complaint and send a voucher to encourage the dissatisfied customer to visit again at a cost of approximately €100. So the 1/10/100 rule could be rewritten as €1/ €10/ €100.

In order to convert dissatisfied customers (who complain) into delighted customers we in DTA Marketing have modified this rule to include a '+1' or *something extra* that is appreciated by the customer. So now the rule is: 1+*1*/10/100.

1+*1*:10:100 Rule = something extra

The following table illustrates the implementation of '+1' ideas. Take our hotel example: each department of the hotel needs to identify '+1' ideas that could be implemented in their area:

1. Situations or complaints where a '+1' is needed.
2. Actions ('+1's) to be taken.

Department	Situation/Problem	Examples of '+1's (examples are taken in no order)
Restaurant	Cold food Long delays Food undercooked Wrong order Table not set right	Complimentary drink Extra garnish on replacement plate No extra charge for steak Change food without question
Bar	Slow service Wrong order Bad pint Cracked glass	Free drink Free hot nuts Free crisps
Accommodation/ Reception	Room not ready Need to change room TV broken Needs more towels Smoke in room	'VIP' room — flowers/fruit/mineral water Complimentary tea/coffee in the bar while waiting the room Provide more biscuits (on the table in the room)
Leisure Centre	Resident doesn't have a cap No towels Sauna/steam room broken Children in adults' only time	Free loan of cap Complimentary cap or goggles Free drink from the machine

It is vitally important to record what the complaint was about and the '+1' solution provided.

A dissatisfied customer can be converted back to a satisfied customer if the complaint is resolved. If *something extra* is done, it is likely that the customer will be pleased, even delighted. Each company should identify what extra items/ services could be given to the customer to convert dissatisfied customers into delighted customers.

Case Study — Dorchester Hotel moves to boost its world-class reputation

At London's Dorchester Hotel, Personnel and Training Manager David Lowth faced the challenge of having to improve what was already excellent service.

'Our aim was to be one of the top five hotels in the world' he says. 'We had to build on a reputation which was already very high. We were known for excellent service and our customers come to us with very high expectations indeed. One of our challenges was working out how to exceed those expectations.'

At a top management weekend brainstorming session a number of action points were agreed.

The first was to extend the induction period for new staff from one day to five and to run it as soon as a new member of staff arrived at the hotel. The five days would cover the Dorchester's philosophy, markets and service culture as well as its systems and procedures. This simple change has already brought a new generation of staff to the hotel that is eager and ready to challenge non-productive behaviour.

The team's second action point was to set up and agree service standards in each of the hotel's 30 departments.

The third was to establish ten service standards, which would apply throughout the organisation.

The ten generic standards are now on display everywhere on the staff side of the Dorchester and each department has standards of its own in place. Members of senior management are practising a coaching style of leadership and people are joining the hotel with a new understanding of service. Out of the numerous awards the Dorchester has recently won, the staff is most proud of its Egon Ronay 'Hotel of the Year' award and being named 'Hotel with the Friendliest Welcome' by the readers of Executive Travel.

Key service standards:
- always make eye contact and acknowledge the customer's presence
- always personally escort the customer to the area or outlet required
- always make an effort to find out and use the customer's name
- always give your complete attention to the customer
- always be visible and open to the customer's needs
- always ensure customers are dealt with promptly
- always keep commitments made to the customer
- always see the task through to completion
- always exceed the customer's expectations
- always check for customer satisfaction.

Source: *Hotel & Catering Magazine*

It is no accident that the ten general standards that the hotel has adopted all began with the world 'always'. 'When you are working for world-class service' says David Howth, 'consistency of delivery is paramount. Consistency is the key'.

It is vital to aim high — to delight not just satisfy. Dissatisfied customers can be turned into delighted customers if their complaint is resolved quickly and something extra is given to compensate for the inconvenience caused and to show that the complaint was a rare occurrence.

Customers love to hear their name used — it makes them feel like a regular customer and that their custom is appreciated.

Key customer care strategies

- Aim to delight customers.
- Treat all customers as though they are lifetime customers.
- Make sure your customers know about your unique selling points.
- Analyse the 'moments of truth' and make improvements.
- Turn casual customers into regular customers.
- Welcome the stranger.
- Deal with complaints quickly.
- Go beyond what is expected when fixing complaints.

Chapter Six

Improving Customer Care Standards

- Measure existing customer care standards before introducing higher standards.

- Set and agree standards with staff.

- Golden rule: never lose a customer.

- Consult staff and customers on ways to improve customer care.

- Explain purpose of improvements in customer care to staff or they will visit the 'valley of excuses'.

- Display agreed standards of customer care in appropriate places.

Figures are your history — customers are your present and your future.

Philip Kotler

It is quite difficult to set and maintain high customer care standards. In what areas should they be set? Will staff agree to the standards? How will we know that these standards will be maintained even if the manager is not there?

These are some of the many questions you might ask about implementing higher standards of customer care. So where do you start? I suggest you measure where you are now so that you know the level of customer care you are providing. When you know the level you are at, you can then set about improving it.

IDENTIFYING KEY CUSTOMER CARE AREAS

Before measurement is carried out it will be necessary to decide on the key customer care areas that you are going to focus on. It will be different for each company depending on the industry sector and ethos of the company.

Key areas for setting standards in customer care include the following:
- telephone
- staff friendliness
- personal appearance
- tidiness of reception
- accuracy
- speed of service
- complaint handling
- correspondence
- product knowledge
- personal hygiene

- work standard
- cleanliness of facilities
- response rate.

Various department stores have a printed message to their customers on the back of their till receipts with conditions for returning goods etc. Here is an example of this type of practice.

Our Guarantee of Satisfaction

We want you to be happy with everything you buy at Debenhams. If you are not happy with your unused purchase feel free to return it for an exchange or refund.

Items with proof of purchase will be exchanged or refunded by the original method of payment. Items without proof of purchase will be exchanged or refunded in the form of gift vouchers.

Please keep your receipt to speed up the process. This does not affect the statutory rights of Debenhams.

Source: Back of Debenham's till receipts

Stew Leonard, owner of one of the most successful supermarkets in America, put a 3,000kg granite rock outside the entrance to his store with the words:

Rule 1: The customer is always right.
Rule 2: If the customer is ever wrong, re-read rule no.1.

The customer care ethos of a company will provide guidance on the areas to be measured and improved. The key to selecting areas for measurement (customer care standards) is to identify those areas that will make a noticeable difference to the customer, for example have a brainstorming session with staff to identify these areas. Review customer complaints and make sure the problem areas are included in the customer care standards. Staff appearance is very important in a retail outlet but not perhaps as vital in a back office job.

Organising customer service — questions that need attention

1. What do our customers want?
2. Are we delivering a good service?
3. How do we compare with competitors in terms of customer care?
4. Have we set standards?
5. Have we trained in customer service?
6. What are the key contact points with customers ('moments of truth')?
7. Have we measured customer service?

There are a number of steps that can be taken to improve customer care. These are:

1. Identifying key customer care areas.
2. Setting standards with staff.
3. Measuring customers' perception of these areas (benchmark).
4. Training staff in customer care.
5. Identifying areas for improvement and actions to be taken.
6. Implementing standards and devising customer care action plan.
7. Again measuring customers' perception of the customer care standards.
8. Retraining and refocusing staff on key customer care issues.

Another approach to identifying areas is to evaluate the needs of customers. What are their specific needs from a customer care point of view? For instance, customers of a butcher's shop will want the staff to be knowledgeable about the meat as well as being able to make cooking suggestions and also to practice high standards of hygiene. In an insurance brokerage, customers expect a speedy reply to queries, fast payment of claims, accuracy etc.

A 'Cycle of Service' model (see Chapter 5) can be used to set out all the 'moments of truth'. An analysis of the 'moments of truth' will also provide ideas for further thinking and in turn help to identify the customer care standards.

I suggest these key areas are identified and discussed with staff. Ideally all staff should be involved and this is easier if it is a small or medium sized company. In larger companies it might be more appropriate to form a customer care team to discuss these issues.

You can identify key customer care areas by:
• reviewing developments in your industry sector
• evaluating the specific needs and expectations of your customers
• assessing company ethos towards customers
• examining the 'moments of truth'.

Forget about what you want to do and focus on what your customer wants.

SETTING STANDARDS WITH STAFF

If members of staff are not involved in this process it will not be effective. I once heard of a company that formed a team for setting these company customer care standards. They even had a booklet printed for all the staff with company logos and the company slogan on the front. It set out the standards and included a message from the chairman. When the staff came in after a weekend they found this booklet on their desks and didn't really know what to do with it. Most put it away in a drawer, some put it in their in-tray with the intention of digesting it later. But they didn't feel ownership for the standards nor were they going to implement many of the suggestions. So it didn't work!

In my experience getting staff (or staff representatives) involved is critical as it will encourage staff to have ownership of the standards.

The key is to take staff through a number of customer care concepts and explain the role customer care has in differentiating their products from their competitors. You will be surprised how high the standards will be set by staff for themselves when they believe in the competitive advantage that can be gained. Most staff will be surprised at the value of a lifetime customer.

There are numerous examples of this. The staff in a butcher's shop in Carlow have agreed that all the members of staff must shower before coming to work thereby showing respect for each other and also because they are aware of the close proximity of customers to them. Members of staff at Advance Pitstop have suggested that every staff member gives some safety advice to each customer after they have had their car examined, repaired or serviced. If staff aim to deliver a certain standard of service they are likely to succeed most of the time and customers will notice the difference.

MEASURING CUSTOMERS' PERCEPTION OF AGREED STANDARDS

Unless you know where you stand in relation to the customer's viewpoint, it is difficult to know if you are improving or disimproving your standard of customer care. Measurement or benchmarking (a measurement at a point in time) should be carried out on a regular basis. Bank of Ireland carry out customer satisfaction surveys on three occasions during the year. Each year the target is raised so that performance improves. Branch managers must produce a plan for actions to be taken in the area of customer care.

The methods of measurement include:
- customer satisfaction surveys, e.g. questionnaires (with rating questions enclosed) — postal/personal interview
- comment cards
- mystery shoppers.

These methods were discussed in detail in Chapter 4.

> Look at the business though the customers' eyes.
>
> *Source*: Dr Aidan Daly, Head of Marketing, University College Galway

In many instances, members of staff believe that they are competent at providing the service to customers and that the customers are quite happy with the service. Often it is only when researched figures are presented which show that the customers' perception of the service provided are below what is expected do staff realise there is a problem. In cases like this you will have the undivided attention of staff for training sessions and for setting higher standards.

TRAINING STAFF IN CUSTOMER CARE CONCEPTS

Many companies organise training courses for staff in key customer care concepts. Unless these concepts were explained before, most members of staff are not aware of:
- the value of a lifetime customer
- the financial loss due to dissatisfied customers
- the need to 'delight' customers

- the power of superior customer care as a marketing tool
- the need to fix up complaints quickly.

(The above concepts are explained throughout the book.)

This focus on customer care is often quite new to staff, especially younger staff, and it needs time to sink in. It is often really useful to share the results of the customer satisfaction survey with staff to emphasis how good or bad the service is. The results might surprise some of the staff who probably think they are providing a top class service to customers.

Many companies don't 'walk the talk' when it comes to customer service, they talk about it but they don't put it into action.

Source: Ian Kingston, Essential Training

Lifetime value of the customer

Delighted customer (e.g. supermarket customer) spends €100 per week x 50 weeks x 10 years = €50, 000.

Delighted customer tells three others who become lifetime customers = €150,000 (50,000 x 3)

Loss of lifetime customer

Dissatisfied customer will not return and not spend €50,000. Instead they tell ten others not to shop there (€50,000 x 10) = €500, 000 potential loss.

Golden rule: never lose a customer.

IDENTIFYING AREAS FOR IMPROVEMENT AND ACTIONS TO BE TAKEN

The best ideas for improving customer care in a company are likely to come from staff and customers. Members of staff know about the products and services in considerable depth and, if consulted, could provide clever suggestions for improving the way the company deals with customers. In addition, they can identify areas where customers are displeased with the service, e.g. opening hours, out of stocks etc. It is good practice to have regular brainstorming sessions with staff on a variety of topics. I suggest you always include customer care on the agenda.

Management and staff should visit competitors (at home or abroad) like a 'busman's holiday' (as it is known) and gather ideas from what they observe and hear.

In the Station House Hotel in the West of Ireland, a staff member suggested that they should put a note in all the bathrooms to explain that the slightly discoloured water was in fact perfectly pure and hygienic and that the colour was natural and came from the nearby mountain. Another staff suggestion was to put a personal welcome note and luxury sweets from the manager on every guest's bed.

Staff will also hear suggestions from customers who would like to see improvements. Comments like 'I wish you could...' or 'Why don't you...?' are quite common. In a brainstorming environment such comments should be recalled.

Customers are experts

Customers are probably the best source of ideas for improving customer care — naturally! They have probably tried your competitors as well and in many cases visited the same kind of operation while abroad.

The following are a good source of ideas for improving customer care:

- customers
- staff
- visits to competitors
- visits to international competitors
- competitors' websites
- international and trade magazines
- specialist customer care publications and books
- customer care training courses
- customer care specialists.

There are a number of methods used to gather these suggestions. These include:

1. Customer comment cards (make room for their comments as well as ratings).
2. Market research (include a question such as: 'How can we improve the service we provide?').
3. One to one (ask a direct question during an informal discussion on customer care issues).
4. Staff ideas can be encouraged by having a 'staff suggestion box' (and reward). For innovative suggestions an 'ideas board' (white board) could be introduced where staff write down their idea and it is discussed at the next department meeting.
5. Management by walking about (MBWA as Peters and Waterman call it) and by observing customers in action — this will generate some new ideas.

> ### Customer care on the management agenda
>
> Customer issues should be discussed at the weekly management meeting. In every Jurys Doyle Hotel customer care is on the agenda and feedback from comment cards and complaints are discussed.

Customer care needs to be managed and taken as a priority if you intend making it a key part of your strategy to attract and hold customers.

As already mentioned, visiting your competitors at home and abroad is a good source of generating ideas for improving customer care. Each year five executives from Superquinn Supermarkets visit America for the Food Marketing Institutes's (FMI) annual convention in Chicago (it takes three days to visit all the exhibition halls). After the convention they also visit the leading supermarkets in other cities to gather as many ideas as possible. It would be normal for this team to collect about 35 ideas which can be implemented (from a list of over 60 initial concepts) on the annual trip.

> ### Chartbusters newsletter
>
> Chartbusters produce a free monthly magazine for customers. For each video, they inform customers about: release dates, running time = 119 mins, satellite holdback = 1 year, TV holdback = 2 years. In this way they go beyond what is expected and provide customers with interesting information.

> One of the key secrets to improving customer care in your company is to see what is happening elsewhere and if appropriate adopt that concept to your industry and your company.

Five Ps of customer service

1. Be *proud:* have confidence in yourself and the job you do.
2. Be *professional:* always put the customer first.
3. Be *polite:* customers deserve respect and consideration.
4. Be *prompt:* never keep a customer waiting.
5. Be *personal:* treat customers as individuals.

Source: *First Rate Customer Service Newsletter* (The Economic Press). Visit their website at www.epinc.com

---

'Valley of Excuses'

On first impressions it could be assumed that if you train staff in customer care techniques and agree higher standards of customer care, the level of customer care in the organisation will increase. This is not always the case.

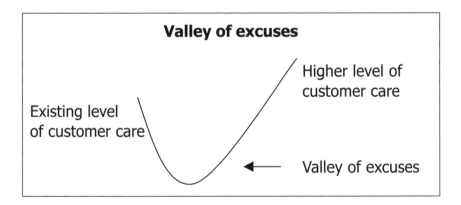

For some staff it will not be easy to change from the 'old ways' to some new modern approach you might have. 'What's wrong with the way we do it now, the customers think we are great?' is a comment you will often hear.

 If the reason for the behavioural change is not properly

explained, staff might be inclined to give excuses why they should not change. When a behavioural change in staff is needed to improve the level of service provided, some staff will resist the new activity as they do not want change. They go, figuratively speaking, into what we in DTA Marketing call the 'valley of excuses'. In other words, they make excuses why they will not implement the change or readjust their behaviour.

Take the customer care idea of using the telephonist's name on the telephone, e.g. 'Good morning, O'Reilly Insurance, Siobhán speaking'. Some staff will resist and say 'the greeting is too long' or 'customers will interrupt me'. I suggest you explain why the change will have benefits for the company — how the staff will appear more friendly, customers will use telephonist's name and feel the company is more personal. Customers will enjoy knowing who specifically they are talking to and the relationship will become more personal. Get the telephonists to try the new initiative a few times and see the reaction.

It is likely, if the customer care initiative is worthwhile, that customers will notice the change and like it. This will encourage the telephonist to use their name all the time and afterwards wonder what all the fuss was about in the first place.

Introducing change in customer care behaviour is not easy but it is very rewarding when it has been successfully implemented and customers do react in a positive manner.

Customer care is what you do after you do what you are expected to do.

Source: Dermot McConkey, Essential Training

IMPLEMENTING STANDARDS AND DEVISING CUSTOMER CARE ACTION PLANS

When customer care standards have been agreed, it is advisable to set them out for all staff to see on a regular basis. A booklet is a good idea. Signs in the staff canteen will be quite visible. Some companies have even printed the standards on their computer mouse mats.

Everyone must know what is expected of them. Some companies tell their customers what levels of customer care they can expect from staff. This is often used as a marketing tool but it will only be effective if the published standards are consistently being met. It would be a disaster if members of staff were not fully aware or committed to the standards and these published standards were not being met. Customers, instead of being pleased with the service supplied, could now be disappointed that promises were not kept.

A plan of action for implementing customer care is needed. It might be advisable to allocate this responsibility to one executive to make sure that the plan is drawn up, agreed and implemented.

Make standards visible

Superquinn demonstrate their standards by giving rewards to customers if they fail to match what is expected. They have signs that inform customers that if you spot a 'goof' as they call it or a customer care mistake (e.g. food out of date, long checkout queue when some checkouts are closed), they will give you free Superclub points.

An action plan could include the following:

1. Make staff more aware of customer care standards and actions.
2. Gather feedback from customers on these standards.
3. Identify specific activities for each area of the business.
4. Regularly carry out customer care training for staff.
5. Use customer care for part of the marketing programme.

Customer care has been used in different ways by companies to promote their products and services. Texaco petrol stations use customers to monitor their standards of customer care by promising 100 per cent satisfaction guaranteed. Customers are invited to complain at the petrol station if they are not 100 per cent satisfied. This is very open — the standards are not set in stone — so it is up to the customer to decide if they are satisfied or not. It also assumes that they are prepared to complain about it if they are dissatisfied.

First Call Direct, the direct home and motor insurance division of Allianz Church & General, have taken a different approach. Each year customers receive a summary of their policy details but also John Betty, their customer services manager, writes to customers with details of the standards. The service commitments are set out with specific targets for First Call Direct to reach.

First Call Direct — our commitment to you

Dear Customer,

The service commitment set out below are the targets we expect to achieve. We hope you will agree that they represent a high level of service.

Phone Service:
- we will give on the spot quotations for home or private motor insurance in the majority of cases
- you are guaranteed friendly and professional service in all your future dealings with us
- we will answer all phone calls within fifteen seconds
- we will return to 'holding' calls at least every 45 seconds
- if you leave a message for someone your call will be returned that day
- all staff will give their name when answering the phone.

Post and Correspondence Service:
- we will issue documentation that is straightforward and easy to understand
- we will issue standard quotations on the same day
- non-standard quotations will be issued within 24 hours of receiving all the required documentation
- we will issue home and motor policies within 48 hours of receiving all documentation from you
- we will make policy alterations and issue relevant documentation within 48 hours of instruction
- standard renewals will be issued at least two weeks prior to your renewal date
- your letters will be acknowledged or replied to within two days of being received.

Property Damage Claims Service — Home and Motor:
- a fast efficient claims service is guaranteed from First Call Direct
- report forms will be issued within 24 hours of being requested
- inspections will be carried out within two working days of you notifying us of where/when damage to your home or car can be inspected
- we will confirm our agreed repair figures within a further two days
- we will issue a settlement cheque to you within three working days of our receipt of all completed documentation.

Let us know what you think.

As a customer you will receive a service evaluation card each time you deal with us. This allows you the opportunity to comment on our service and helps us deliver the service you want. If you have a complaint please contact 1850 213213. I will be happy to talk to you and deal with any complaint that you have.

Many thanks,

John Betty
Customer Services Manager

Source: letter to customers

REPEATING THE MEASUREMENT OF CUSTOMER CARE STANDARDS

It is important to keep measuring what the customers' perception is of the standard of customer care that is provided. Any deterioration needs immediate attention and action.

It is difficult to maintain high standards of customer care unless it is measured. Since it is the customers' perception of how the standard is being maintained, it is important we ask them on a regular basis. It is very easy for standards to slip and all sorts of excuses will be offered up by staff such as 'we have more clients than last year' or 'price is more important than customer care' etc.

Internal competitions are an enjoyable yet practical way of keeping up the high standards of customer care. If there are several outlets, stores or departments it should be easy enough to organise a competition between them to find the 'best at customer care' in the group. The rules of the competition should be clear and it is advisable to use 'mystery shoppers' as the judges. Make the prizes attractive and have the competition over several months so that staff get used to providing these high levels of customer care even if it is only for the competition. It might become a habit.

For instance, BMW customers fill out a questionnaire after they purchase a new car and send it to head office. They are asked to evaluate the service provided by the dealership and the sales staff. The responses are monitored and feedback is provided to the dealership.

RETRAINING AND REFOCUSING STAFF

Customer care is forever — there is never a time when it is completed!

Source: Conor McCarthy, Chairman, Ryan Hotel Group

Customer care can be a fad if you do not put the effort into it. It is easy to forget it for a while and focus on other things. Customer care needs constant attention and focus. Staff will ignore or relax their attention to customer care unless they are driven by senior management. The person with responsibility for customer care in an organisation needs to constantly drive the programme, maintain the standards and, if necessary, retrain and refocus staff.

New members of staff need to be inducted into the company's ethos and approach to customer care. In Superquinn new staff (including part-timers) must attend a three-day course before they learn retailing skills or assist on the shop floor. This induction training will ensure that the customer care ethos and culture is maintained no matter which staff member attends a customer.

As new concepts in customer care keep emerging it is vital that staff are up to date with the latest thinking on customer expectation and customer service requirements. Members of staff need to be refreshed, re-energised and constantly motivated to keep up the high standards of customer care. Visits to competitors' outlets or retail units of companies with a high reputation for customer care will be very valuable for staff to enable them see how others do it.

We should encourage staff serving customers to always look on the positive side. If a customer requests something out of the ordinary, we are inclined to say 'we can't do that because ...'. Instead take a positive view and say 'we will look into it and see how we can do that'. Customers will react favourably to staff if their outlook is proactive and positive rather than negative and dismissive.

Implementing an improved customer care culture takes time. It will not happen overnight no matter how many talks and training sessions are given. It is worthwhile to persist though since customer care can create that competitive edge, and it is not easy to copy and implement.

> Customer care must be implemented with a passion if it is to succeed.

INTERNAL CUSTOMERS

It is easier for front line staff to focus on the customer as they are always present and any issues that arise must be fixed instantly. However, with back office staff or head office the customer is slightly removed.

Superquinn head office is referred to as the support office as it is recognised that its role is to support the stores in their efforts to provide a superior service to customers.

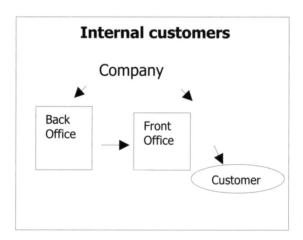

Often front line staff will complain that they do not get enough support internally to carry out their work to the high standards that they would wish. You will often hear: 'it will take months for the IT guy to change the system', 'it's the purchasing officer's fault that we are out of stock', 'the finance people are imposing rules that are not friendly to customers' etc.

In many cases the reason why back office staff do not support the front line team is that they are not directly affected by the customer nor do they see the difficulties or irritation caused by their actions (or inaction). The back office staff need to be fully committed to the customer care ethos if the company as a whole is to provide superior customer care. They need to be trained and perhaps spend some time serving the customer directly.

The back office staff have to realise that they do in fact have direct customers (internal customers), e.g. staff in the branches or stores and that in turn their customers have customers (end customers), i.e. shoppers, who are affected by their actions.

A company that accepts the concept of superior customer care needs to have all staff — those directly and indirectly involved with end customers — focused on providing the best service possible.

Everyone is a link in the supply chain of customer care

Back office staff need to swap roles with front office staff to experience where each other's support is needed and to understand the nature of 'internal customer'.

In car repair garages, there are often complaints that the mechanics cannot understand the repair or servicing instructions from the service advisors on the reception desk. In a BMW dealership they swapped roles for a short while and it really made a difference!

Sometimes we have to experience the difficulties our actions cause to fully appreciate the situation.

Summary

It is important to identify the key areas where customer care can make an impact on customer relations. Set standards for these areas so staff know what to do in the situation. Measurement is vital as staff and management need to know how the customer service is perceived by customers. Staff need to be involved in setting the standards otherwise it will be seen as more instructions from management. Ask customers for ideas on ways to improve the service and customer care.

Change will be difficult to introduce so involve staff and explain the purpose not just the actions required. Internal customers need to be treated as though they are end customers. If everyone in the company is focused on customers, a noticeable difference will be recognised by customers and they will return and purchase more.

Remember the golden rule of customer care: *never lose a customer.*

Key customer care strategies

- Identify areas for setting standards.
- Involve staff in setting customer care standards.
- Regularly monitor the standards.
- Focus on internal customers.
- Train and retrain staff in customer care.
- Devise customer care action plans.

Chapter Seven

Staff — The Key to Success

- Customers often 'buy' staff first before they buy products or services.

- Use customer care and staff in the marketing of your business.

- Selection and motivation of staff is vital where customer care is a key ingredient in your company's offering to customers.

- Staff retention is crucial to a company's success.

- Treat staff like customers.

It is the willingness of people to give themselves over and above the demands of the job that distinguishes the great from the merely adequate organisation.

Peter F Drucker, Management Consultant

The fifth 'P' — people — is probably the most important part of the marketing mix from a differentiating point of view. Products and prices can be quite similar and easily matched by competitors but the way a company looks after customers can vary considerably.

Members of staff are the 'people' concerned and how they enjoy their job and are motivated is vital if they are to have a positive attitude towards customers. If customer care is to be a key part of a company's marketing and selling strategy, there must be considerable investment in staff.

It takes a long time to train staff to become customer focused. Training is needed as customer focused behaviour does not happen naturally. It is difficult to maintain high standards.

There are two key aspects to utilising staff as part of the marketing mix:

1. People 'buy' people first. The impression that staff give to potential customers will significantly influence whether they purchase or not. Staff with a healthy, friendly and positive attitude will certainly impress customers. In many cases customers don't see the actual service itself (accountancy is a case in point) so if they trust and respect the service provider, they 'buy' that person.
2. Customers leave because of indifferent, rude and unhelpful staff. The largest cause of customers leaving companies is because of staff. It may be the policies and practices that are implemented by staff that cause difficulties but staff may get blamed.

Staff can 'make' or 'break' an organisation, yet at times it is very difficult to attract the right kind of staff. When the economy of the country is achieving significant growth, graduates and employees are quite ambitious and in many cases are not prepared to work in demanding yet lowly paid positions. The hotel and catering sector are finding it very difficult to attract staff and frequently are looking abroad for members of staff who are prepared to work and complete their English language studies at the same time. It can be difficult for customers if staff don't understand what the customer is ordering or are unable to answer queries.

Recruitment of the right staff and retaining those staff is crucial for the success of companies. These issues will be dealt with later in the chapter.

Companies that do retain their staff for many years do gain a competitive advantage. Repeat guests who stay at Parknasilla Hotel in Kerry are often greeted by their first name by staff when they return, and are welcomed like long lost cousins!

> Superior customer care cannot be copied overnight by competitors.

Staff are the first contact a customer has when visiting a company's premises, e.g. receptionists, sales staff. When a potential customer telephones a company it is a staff member who will give the first impression of the company. The greeting they receive will create an immediate impression.

Disney and Warner Brothers' retail outlets have a 'greeter' at the entrance to their shops just to say 'hello and welcome' to each individual as they enter the premises. While some customers may see this as a gimmick, since so few shops bother with this greeting, it is a noticeable difference when compared to competitors.

A company that is steeped in a strong customer care culture will be noticeably different and better than one that is only trying to appear customer orientated and lacks the real conviction and belief in the competitive advantage of superior customer care. True customer orientated companies have hundreds of examples of the way they treat customers and will easily pass any customer care test!

Senator Feargal Quinn believes that you can teach a nice person to be a good shop assistant but you cannot teach a good shop assistant to be a nice person! Staff selection is critical if you want members of staff who are customer focused.

Customer focused organisations select and train their staff with customer care foremost in their thinking. Members of staff are motivated and probably rewarded based on their commitment to customer care and this is evidenced by their actions. Staff know instinctively what to do whenever customers complain or have any kind of difficulty. They are empowered to act on their own initiative.

Happy members of staff give very positive signals to existing and potential customers. They are likely to be enjoying their work probably because of the management's attitude, working with quality products in pleasant surroundings and having rewarding and motivating salary structures. If staff like their environment then maybe the customers will also!

Customer needs will vary

Staff need to:
• listen
• question
• observe
so that they can deal with each customer in the best possible manner.

INTERNAL CUSTOMERS

> If you are not directly serving customers, you need to be serving someone who is.
>
> *Source*: Jan Carlzon, SAS Airlines

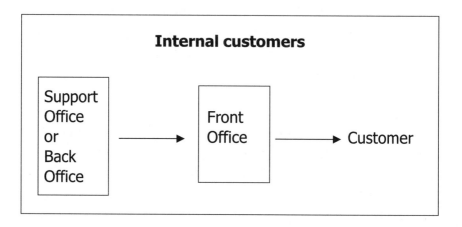

Internal customers

Support Office or Back Office → Front Office → Customer

All members of staff in an organisation need to be focused on the customer. There should be no 'them' and 'us' in an organisation. Head office or the back office and front line staff need to work together to meet customers' needs.

Too often in an organisation the front line staff are let down by systems, procedures and policies which are often controlled by back office staff. It is important that every staff member understands the needs of customers. Rotating jobs can be quite valuable as someone new to that job can bring new ideas and approaches. It also makes staff aware of the pressures and responses needed when dealing directly with customers.

The following are key points for improving internal staff relations:

- set internal customer care standards
- cross-functional teams
- job exchanges/rotation

- open and honest reviews
- regular communication.

Internal customer care standards

Some companies set internal customer care standards as well as external customer care standards to ensure that all sections of the company are focused on customers (both internal and external). It can be very demotivating for staff if some are being monitored and rewarded for their customer care approach while others seemingly are not customer orientated at all.

Cross-functional teams

Cross-functional teams can be very effective in resolving customer care issues as well as educating back office staff to the needs and requirements of customers. This provides staff with an opportunity to meet and listen to other staff members. Cross-functional teams are often formed to solve problems and plan new approaches to looking after customers.

Job exchanges/rotation

Many companies swop staff around — a sort of 'work experience' — to another department or branch. In this way they will understand the pressures of other jobs and gain a greater understanding of customers, their changing needs as well as getting ideas for improving the service to customers.

Open and honest reviews

Internal staff surveys, either formal questionnaires or informal discussions, can be very informative for senior management to check the 'pulse' of the organisation. Unhappy staff members are not likely to provide a customer-focused service.

MARKETING YOUR STAFF

Some companies in their advertising and promotions highlight the quality or interest of their staff in their customers' well-being or enjoyment, e.g. airlines, banks etc.

Fitzpatricks Hotel Group mention in their radio campaign that some recent innovations are the result of their staff suggestion programme. A recent radio advertisement for a direct insurance company included a sample recording of how they answer the telephone which included using the words: 'Hello, Guardian Insurance, Mary speaking, how may I help you?' It certainly gives an impression that the company is customer orientated.

On the dinner menu at Hotel Westport the name of the chef who cooked the meal is mentioned. On most aeroplane flights you are introduced to the captain and crew by name. In the British Airways' magazine, I read an article by one of their pilots who said his role was not only to ensure that the plane landed safely but also that everyone enjoyed the flight. Have you noticed that pilots are taking a greater interest in passengers and from time to time suggest we look out our windows to see views of famous cities as we pass overhead.

On Singapore Airlines every passenger is addressed by name. The customers' names are on the passenger list (by seat) for most airlines but Singapore Airlines choose to use the customer's name and therefore make an impact.

British Airways demonstrate their commitment to reducing the hassle of checking in at airports and increase passengers' comfort by introducing innovative changes. Their concept is: 'Your time is a precious commodity, we promise to keep it that way' and staff members demonstrate how they can help.

Winning awards can create positive publicity for customer-orientated companies. TSB Bank helpdesk won the 'Best Helpdesk of the Year' award at the annual call centre awards ceremony, which was excellent for staff morale. Winning awards is motivating for staff as well as a clear demonstration to existing and potential customers that they are a leading company in their area of expertise and are a customer-orientated company.

The Ryan Hotel Group won the Irish travel agents' 'Best Hotel Group of the Year' award five times running!

If you have a choice of suppliers and one of them empathises with you while the other shows no interest, you will go for the one who is nice. It may only be that they remembered your face and smiled, but it makes all the difference.

Source: John McInerney, Senior Specialist, Irish Management Institute

---

STAFF IDEAS

Next to customers, members of staff are probably the most valuable source of ideas. They are most familiar with what customers like and need and they also hear from customers how things can be improved. For some staff these ideas will go straight over their heads while others will take note of the exceptional ideas and suggest their implementation.

Companies should encourage staff to act on their own initiative when it comes to dealing with customers. This is where training plays a crucial role. Yet, we have all heard of staff being fired for assisting clients because they broke some rule in the process!

Staff ideas need to be encouraged. Some companies have staff suggestion boxes in their canteens and particularly good suggestions will get a monetary award.

You can encourage staff ideas by:
- having a staff suggestion box
- rewarding staff initiative
- recognising staff initiatives at appraisal time
- sending staff on courses

- encouraging staff to read international publications and search the Internet.

While Des Burke Kennedy of Advance Pitstop was enjoying one of his passions in life — commentating on the Waterskiing World Championships in Australia — he decided to take a helicopter ride and get in some sightseeing. When he booked the trip for an early morning start, the receptionist recognised his accent and mentioned that they had an Irish pilot who was scheduled for the afternoon trip and would he like to change the time of his trip. He declined due to time commitments but she, using her own initiative and customer friendly approach, persuaded the Irish pilot to take the 7.00 a.m. trip and surprised Des the next day.

He was delighted and while he may not be a repeat customer, he certainly spread the word among his colleagues at the championship and consequently, that company is likely to attract more visitors. It is likely that the management of this sightseeing helicopter firm didn't even know about the change in the pilots' schedule but the firm has gained from a staff member's initiative and customer focus.

At appraisal time, it should be noted if a staff member showed initiative and made innovative suggestions during the year. Staff should know that it is part of their job to come up with new ideas and suggest interesting approaches to the way the business is being run. Equally, there must be fair reward and recognition for their efforts.

CHECKLISTS

The quality of work and interest in the job will vary with each staff member. In fact this is the big problem with staff — the variety of attitudes and inconsistency of focus. This highlights the need for customer care training.

One of the solutions that companies use is checklists. If each staff member adheres to the agreed checklist then it is likely that customers will receive the same level of service from each staff member. Have you ever gone to a restaurant and hoped you were allocated a particular waiter or waitress as they were very friendly and efficient the last time? I'm sure you have.

It would be ideal if all staff delivered this high level of customer service. Superior customer care comes from:

- strong leaders
- good systems
- checklists that staff adhere to
- a passionate commitment to delighting the customer.

The key ingredient is training. The owner or senior executives need to be fully committed to delivering high standards of customer service if it is to work.

The Studio Restaurant in Kiev, Ukraine has incredible standards of customer care. When asked how they managed to serve everyone's food to the right customer without having to interrupt the customer, the waiter modestly replied: 'it's my job'. But they do have a system that all staff follow and it is very successful. Have you witnessed a waiter interrupting a group of customers having dinner to call 'who's the chicken?' and 'who's the duck?'? Such a simple task, you would imagine it would be easy to take notes or even remember who ordered what.

> Consistent levels of customer service require:
>
> 1. Training: in customer care concepts and customer orientation.
> 2. Checklists: make sure all the agreed activities are completed.
> 3. Commitment: by owners/managers as well as staff.
> 4. Leadership: senior executives should lead by example.
> 5. Systems: listening systems are needed to capture comments from customers and staff.

STAFF RECRUITMENT

When people are the key ingredient in your company, it is vital you attract and select the most suitable candidates for the job. Before you advertise, it is important that not only is a job specification set out but also a person profile. The new team member will have to fit in with existing staff and also be someone that will proudly represent the company to customers.

In Superquinn, where the focus is on superior customer service, the interview will focus on the candidate's people skills and in particular, how easily and often they smile! Superquinn's view is that if they get the right person they will train them in the operational skills later.

It can be very difficult sometimes to attract staff especially when the economy is experiencing high growth. Companies have to make an impression in their recruitment advertising in order to attract the right calibre of candidates for the job. Many companies are advertising on the radio in order to attract potential candidates.

The images or script in an advertisement will often provide potential candidates with an indication of the type of company that is recruiting, but more importantly will demonstrate their focus (or lack of it) on staff and customers.

> We want to turn uncut diamonds into sparkling gems.
>
> *Source*: H. Samuel Jewellers (recruitment advertisement).

IBM recently advertised in the main section of *The Irish Times* that they were looking for staff and suggested readers look in the business supplement for further details. This was to make sure potential candidates noticed the main advertisement. The theme of the advertisement was 'this is your wake up call'.

In order to attract the right calibre of staff Lucent Technologies ran an open day at The Shelbourne Hotel. Advertisements were placed in the recruitment sections of the national newspapers as well as clever, witty radio commercials in case the newspaper advertisements didn't make an impact.

In an innovative move a British multinational placed advertisements on the sides of Dublin city buses to attract top Irish university graduates.

When recruiting customer care staff, it is their people skills that one should look for. Watch out for evidence in their CV of involvement with customers/people either in a previous job or in their personal life, e.g. scouts, teams, voluntary caring activities etc. Not everyone is suitable to front line work, i.e. dealing directly with customers.

Some companies take induction training very seriously. In customer-orientated companies, it is normal to spend two or three days in initial, introductory training to bring new staff into the customer care culture that already exists in the company. A classic mistake is to take an untrained new staff member and put them straight on the shop floor (especially if there is a shortage of staff) and hope they will act like the longer serving staff. This rarely happens as a customer care ethos does not come naturally to people, especially to younger staff.

Staff need to understand that all their actions have an impact on the perception customers have of the company. Untrained staff may give a bad or poor impression and you may lose customers as a result. Losing a lifetime customer can be very expensive especially if they spread negative word of mouth about your business. It may discourage other potential customers from visiting your premises or dealing with your company.

STAFF MOTIVATION

Treat staff like customers.

Staff members need to be motivated to keep on delivering superior levels of customer care. If staff enjoy their work, they will take on many challenges and respond to customers in a positive manner. How do we motivate and encourage staff? Certainly money is an influence, but as the American psychologist Henry Hertzberg pointed out, there are many ways to motivate staff besides monetary considerations.

Hertzberg developed the 'two-factor theory' of motivation based on research on what motivated workers and also what factors caused dissatisfaction. He found that when certain motivators (achievement, recognition, responsibility, work itself, appreciation, personal growth) were present, workers were highly motivated and satisfied.

People respond well to recognition of their achievements. The owner or boss congratulating a staff member on their achievement, either in work or in their personal time, goes a long way towards encouraging them to keep up the good work and to keep on trying to improve.

Many companies are good at delegating work to employees and giving them recognition for their efforts. Members of staff feel very proud if they are empowered to make decisions and have responsibility for their area. Most staff members enjoy the responsibility of being able to fix customers' complaints without having to ask a manager for permission. It is vital for management to encourage staff to take on this responsibility as quick action is often needed.

A very typical issue under discussion in many companies at the moment is salary increase versus time increase. Many employees are finding that they don't see their partners or children as much as they used to as they spend longer hours at work. Some innovative companies have approached this issue in different ways. Instead of a salary increase, staff may get a time increase (same salary, less hours). Other companies have condensed the working week into four and a half days. Short Brothers in Belfast, now part of Bombardier, have introduced new working hours that encourage employees to finish at 1.00 p.m. on Fridays.

Staff development and partnership

Throughout the year much of my focus has been on in-house structure and staffing issues. I have always stressed that I did not want to build a large office but one that could become very effective and professional. It was important to build morale and engage in staff development so that we had the internal capacity to move forward. The complexities were enormous as there are staff in Geneva, New York and in over 20 field presences on four continents.

In August I welcomed the heads of all our field operations to Geneva for a week long session. This was the first time that such an event had been organised and it proved extremely useful – for those working in the field and in Geneva. It is an activity that I would wish to see happen on a regular, perhaps even a yearly basis.

Source: The UN High Commissioner for Human Rights, Mrs Mary Robinson. Extracts from an article in *The Irish Times* on her first year in office.

Many companies run internal competitions to motivate staff. While most competitions (e.g. 'Station of the Month' between the different petrol stations in a group) can be motivating, individually focused competitions like 'Employee of the Month' can be divisive, as often there is more trouble between staff over a badly organised or unfair competition than no competition at all.

STAFF RETENTION

Having gone to the trouble of recruiting and training staff, then motivating them to keep up these high standards of customer care, it is very frustrating when some of them leave.

Customers get used to certain staff and staff that are interested in their job make an impression on customers. Staff retention is vital if a company wishes to continue the high levels of customer service. Some companies that experience a lot of staff changeovers put staff retention on the agenda of management meetings. It is important to find out why staff members are leaving. If staff morale is low, there can be plenty of staff defections in a short period of time. Of course many leave because they get a better offer, i.e. more money, but there are often many other reasons why they leave which have nothing to do with salary, e.g. low morale, poor career opportunities, no authority to make decisions, poor training etc. If you kept staff turnover figures you might be shocked to discover how high your staff turnover actually is!

SO WHAT CAN BE DONE?

Many large multinational companies, such as banks and computer companies (e.g. Microsoft), give shares or share options to their staff instead of bonuses. This trend is spreading to medium sized Irish companies that intend floating on the Irish Stock Exchange. If staff members are involved in the ownership of the company they are more likely to stay there and also make sure it is a profitable operation.

Further training and education can be a motivator. Some companies have a great reputation for looking after staff and so they will attract high calibre staff and are likely to keep them.

Why do members of staff leave? Exit interviews are very valuable in finding out the thoughts of the staff member who is leaving. Staff in this situation can afford to be honest and open in their views as they have nothing to lose. While the reasons may vary for the different staff members, often it is a case of poor morale or a particular staff member who is causing others to leave. Management need to act fast if there are morale problems as matters normally get worse not better. Exit interviews help top management to 'feel the temperature' of their organisation.

The following are some useful staff retention strategies:

- share in ownership of company
- exit interviews
- regular appraisals
- training
- social activities or staff outings
- staff discounts
- open, clear communication
- regularly discuss staff retention at management meetings
- maintain staff turnover figures.

Well-managed companies carry out two performance appraisals with each staff member on an annual basis. One of the appraisals may also be used for salary review but both should also be used to make sure that the staff member is happy and content in their job and that any issues such as training are identified.

Some companies plan three to five training days for each employee each year, not alone to make sure that they are learning the latest methods and skills, but also to ensure that they are motivated in their job. Training gives staff an opportunity, while away from the company, to take a fresh look at the way the business is run and to come back refreshed, renewed and ready to increase their participation.

'Staff that play together, work better together' — Confucius could have written that! Staff members who enjoy socialising together often have a great rapport in the office during the day. Company outings can be great fun and a way to get to know others better. In particular, it can be very interesting for management to see their staff in a non-work establishment and perhaps see aspects of their characters that would not normally be seen at work.

If the company sells consumer goods or attractive products or services, it is often an incentive to staff to give them a discount. Staff members at Tesco enjoy a 10 per cent discount off their shopping, while airline staff and family can fly at significantly discounted fares. Hotel staff can often use the leisure centre facilities.

The 'mushroom philosophy' of management (keeping staff in the dark about company decisions) is still alive and well in many companies. Staff members usually want to know what is going on and want feedback on their own performance. At Superquinn members of staff are shown the sales and contribution figures for their section on a weekly basis. The trust and confidence of management in their staff is rewarded by the confidential manner in which members of staff treat these figures as well as the interest shown by staff in improving the figures each week.

Company newsletters or internal chatty e-mails can be an ideal solution for communicating staff news and the reasons or background for management decisions to a wider audience. General staff meetings can be very valuable provided there is a clear agenda and the meeting is well chaired. Staff retention is too serious an issue to be left to chance. It needs to be planned and reviewed on a regular basis.

Conclusion

Staff are the key to a company's success. Customers notice staff first when they make contact with a company. Selection and motivation of staff is vital if customer care is part of the marketing strategy.

Key customer care strategies

- Recruit suitable staff for front line positions.
- Focus on staff retention.
- Encourage ideas from staff.
- Motivate staff.

Chapter Eight

Secrets of Customer Care

- Key principles of customer care.

- Suggested actions.

- Implement a system to ensure ideas are executed.

The companies that understand customer needs and deliver superior customer care will have delighted customers.

Delighted customers are very loyal. They tell their friends and they keep coming back, which increases the profitability of the company.

I am setting out below some secrets that I have learnt over the years which I believe will improve your customer service. Relevant examples and suggestions are included. I call them the Ten Commandments of Customer Care.

1. ASK AND DELIVER

> Ask customers what they want and give it to them again and again!

The best source of ideas is the customers themselves. They will set the standards if you will listen to them. Give them what they want and they will come back again and again.

I suggest you:
- ensure customer comment cards are available for customers
- carry out customer research and make sure to ask open questions
- review customer comments at management meetings.

2. UNDERPROMISE AND OVER DELIVER

> Customers expect you to keep your word. Exceed it!

Many companies, unfortunately, do not keep their promises. How many times have you waited in for a delivery that never came? It is obvious that you should be contacted if there is a delay. Customers are delighted when the service is better than

expected. Don't promise that every delivery will be on time —
but do arrive early on occasions!

    I suggest you:

- tell customers in advance if there are problems
- ensure your suppliers deliver on time
- plan backup or emergency options.

3. THE CUSTOMER IS KING — LONG LIVE THE KING!

> Whatever the customer asks, the answer is always 'yes'.

If we make it difficult for the customer or don't respond to
their requests, they will go elsewhere. A company should try
to be flexible rather than have a rigid policy. Customers often
recommend improvements to products or services and if these
are implemented they might attract more customers. If a
customer complains, don't tell them that they are wrong. If
you insult customers they will not return but they will tell their
friends. Treat customers as you would like to be treated yourself
— like a king!

    I suggest you:

- never prove that a customer is wrong
- always be positive
- show respect.

4. I WILL LOOK AFTER THAT

> Every staff member who deals with customers should
> have the authority to handle complaints.

Customers want staff to solve their problem. They don't want
to be passed on to another staff member and have to start
telling their complaint all over again. Members of staff in some

companies are empowered to deal with customer complaints on the spot. If a problem is not dealt with on the spot, it becomes more expensive to resolve the more it is passed up the line.

I suggest you:

- empower staff to fix complaints and offer something extra
- review complaints and fix causes
- revert back to the customer when the complaint is resolved.

5. Encourage complaints

> If your customers tell you what is wrong, you can fix it.

It may seem strange to encourage complaints but there is a considerable benefit to be gained by knowing what is causing the dissatisfaction. The complaints should not be seen as a personal attack on anyone. It may be the case that the system needs changing. Some companies expect everyone to answer the telephones during lunchtime. In most cases nobody does and customers complain. Perhaps a rota is needed to cover lunchtime telephone calls.

I suggest you:

- set up a customer listening system
- put customer complaints on the agenda for management meetings
- check with customers who complain that the complaint was resolved to their satisfaction.

6. Tell what you can do — not what you can't do

> Be positive, be confident and customers will know that they are being listened to, and action will happen.

How often do you hear, 'That's not my job' or 'It's not my fault'. Customers want action and the company that responds and takes responsibility will attract more customers. Customers do not want to hear about your difficulties. Don't say or think, 'We can't do that because ...' instead try to think, 'How can we do that?'

I suggest you:

- use positive not negative language
- tell customers what you have done after listening to their comments
- pass on customer requests to appropriate staff rather than ignore the request.

7. People buy people first

> You must impress your customers because when they buy from the company they get you as well.

First impressions are vital. If you choose a company from the Golden Pages and their telephone manner is rude and unhelpful it is likely you will say 'no thank you' and ring the next company. If the sales person doesn't impress a customer, are they going to trust that company? Staff training is an investment.

I suggest you:

- make sure front office staff are friendly and polite
- train staff in customer communications including the use of body language
- include friendliness as a criteria for selecting front line staff.

8. Customers buy benefits not features

> You should turn the features into benefits for the customer.

Often a company communicates using technical terms that customers are unfamiliar with and as a result they don't see the end benefit. You should make it easy for the customers to buy your products and services by telling them what's in it for them, e.g. the Ryan Hotel Group have 'friendly fellows' to entertain the children so the children really enjoy their holidays and want to go there again the following year. While the children are happy being entertained by the 'friendly fellows' the parents can relax and enjoy their holiday also.

I suggest you:
- review written customer communications for the overuse of technical language
- always explain the product or service features in terms of benefits
- identify the benefits or unique selling points of your company and encourage all staff to use these messages.

9. USE THE CUSTOMER'S NAME WHENEVER POSSIBLE

> Customers like to be recognised and their name to be mentioned.

Doesn't it feel great to walk into a restaurant and the manager says, 'It's nice to see you John and Mary, would you like a table near the window?' To be greeted in this way makes you feel like you are being treated as though you are a king. Some telephone receptionists are very quick to recognise customer's voices and are able to improve the image of the company by addressing the customer by name.

I suggest you:
- identify methods of getting customers' names, including asking them directly!
- encourage front line staff to wear name badges

- learn customers' names and use them before they give or show you their name.

10. I<small>T'S THE DIFFERENCE THAT MAKES A DIFFERENCE</small>

> Superior customer care gives you an opportunity to differentiate your product/service over your competitors.

In order for this to work customers must notice the difference and like it. Some opticians ring their customers a few days after they receive new glasses to see if they are happy with them. Some petrol station assistants clean the car windows, head lamps and windscreen wipers while customers pay for their petrol.

I suggest you:
- identify how you can differentiate your service and implement it
- imagine you are your own customer — what would you like to happen?
- watch for ideas in other industries or sectors.

C<small>ONCLUSION</small>

How can a company improve the level of customer care it provides to its customers?

Strategy — Staff — Systems

The company should decide that customer care will make a difference. Then plan their customer care strategy by identifying the different parts of the service that should be improved.

The staff should be trained and often retrained to ensure they understand the customer care focus and what they have to do to improve the level of service they provide.

Lastly, a system needs to be put in place to ensure that customer-orientated ideas are implemented, monitored and adjusted so that more customers will come back and buy some more.

Remember
**Delighted customers buy regularly
and they tell their friends!**

BOOK SUMMARY

The whole book can be summarised into three key customer care strategies. If you follow these simple concepts you will delight your customers and increase your profits.

1. Never lose a customer.
2. Turn casual customers into regular customers.
3. Treat all customers as though they are potential lifetime customers.

Easy, isn't it!

Good luck.

Workbook

Chapter Nine

Marketing Plans for Profit

- They key part of a marketing plan is the actual planning process.

- The marketing plan is the engine of the company's business plan.

- There are three fundamental questions to be answered in a marketing plan.

- Customer care is a vital part of a marketing plan.

- The action plan must link the marketing objectives and strategies with appropriate actions to be completed by certain dates and by whom.

If you have no plan, any road will take you there.

Many consider writing a marketing plan to be a very time consuming and questionable exercise. Plans are often left on the shelf in the office and only consulted when either sales are below target or an updated plan is required for a board meeting or additional finance is being sought. Sometimes the plan is put away and not seen again until the beginning of the following year.

The marketing plan should be a short, straightforward document and not unduly complicated. It should be aimed at senior management executives as well as those in the marketing department and explain the thinking behind many of the ideas and concepts in the plan as well as containing a description of the current market-place. It concludes with an action plan for marketing programmes and customer care activities.

WHY WRITE A MARKETING PLAN?

The marketing plan should be the blueprint for all the activities of the company for the year ahead. By concentrating on the most productive areas you will also achieve an increase in profits!

If you have no plan, you cannot be sure you are going in the right direction or focusing on the issues to ensure your survival. The most important part of the plan is actually the *planning process* where the activities of the company are reviewed and decisions made about the future.

Customers are the life-blood of a company. The plan will focus on how to attract new customers and how to keep existing customers and which customers, especially lifetime customers, are worth special attention.

PLANNING FOR THE FUTURE OF YOUR COMPANY

Each marketing plan is unique. Your plan relates to your vision of the future for your customers. All relevant people should contribute to it, which ensures *creativity* as well as *ownership* of the plan. There are three stages to writing and implementing a marketing plan. These are:

1. The planning process.
2. Documenting the plan.
3. Implementation and review.

PLANNING PROCESS

The marketing plan is part, some would say a significant part, of the company's business plan. A company's business plan should involve all areas of the company and include manufacturing or operations, finance, personnel, information technology and premises/property.

Before the planning process for the marketing plan begins, information from senior management is required. It is advisable to obtain the 'vision' or 'mission statement' which the board has decided upon. If there is no such statement then the marketing department could propose a mission statement for adoption by the board.

It is likely that there are corporate objectives and targets set out which will provide guidelines on what targets will need to be included in the marketing plan.

Gathering information and carrying out analyses of past performance is a vital part of the planning process. The marketing department is the eyes and ears of the company and it is their role to analyse the marketplace, review trends from a sales and customer point of view and to share these results with other senior executives.

This review and analysis is very important for other senior executives in the company so that they will have a greater understanding of the market and will be better informed. It is more likely that the proposals in the marketing plan will be approved if there is greater understanding of all the issues involved.

It is advisable to consult other senior managers on their ideas, targets, expectations and concerns for the coming year. The plan should involve their input, as the marketing plan must be complementary to and co-ordinated with other plans in the company. All these plans should become integrated into the company's business plan.

Business Plan	
	Finance/Budget
	Manufacturing/ Operations plan
Marketing Plan	
	Personnel/Human Resources plan

The marketing plan could be considered the engine of the business plan because without appropriate products or services and sales the business plan objectives would not be achieved.

DOCUMENTING THE PLAN

At its simplest, there are three fundamental questions to a marketing plan:

1. Where are we now?
2. Where are we going?
3. How are we going to get there?

These questions form a structure which is set out below.

Marketing plan

1. Where are we now?

    1.A.   The Mission Statement
    1.B.   Analysis of marketplace: SWOT analysis, PESTLE analysis[1]
    1.C.   Review past marketing activities
    1.D.   Assess competitors and customer needs

2. Where are we going?

    2.A.   Marketing objectives and goals

3. How are we going to get there?

    3.A.   Marketing strategies
    3.B.   Marketing mix
    3.C.   Marketing and customer care action plan
    3.D.   Budgets and controls

---

[1] Political, Economic, Social, Technological, Legal, Environmental.

> ## Suggested steps for devising a marketing plan
>
> - identify corporate objectives and visions for the future
> - review past sales performance (where did the business come from — products/services, sectors, customers etc.)
> - carry out market-place analysis
> - share information/first draft with relevant colleagues
> - devise objectives, key strategies and sales targets and get input/opinion from relevant colleagues
> - set out action plan, budgets and timetable
> - send marketing plan to senior management for approval.

The Mission Statement

It is important for everyone in the company to know '*What business we are in*?' This is known as the 'Mission Statement' and is often written by the owner/entrepreneur who founded the company.

It should be as broad as possible so that the company is flexible in its outlook and open to grasping opportunities in the marketplace. It should also state the company's main competitive advantage or 'Unique Selling Proposition' (USP). This is usually why the company started in the first place.

Review your present situation

The most important starting point is to carry out a review of '*Where are we now?*' This is popularly known as the SWOT analysis: **S**trengths, **W**eaknesses, **O**pportunities and **T**hreats.

Strengths and weaknesses

A company should be very critical of itself and identify its internal strengths and weaknesses. An internal strength may be that your staff are customer focused, that your products are Irish made or that you provide a 'local' taxi-service. On the other hand a weakness may be that the sales staff are technical people who lack selling skills or that you are dependent on one large customer.

Opportunities and threats

You should look at external opportunities in the marketplace and the threats that may affect your company now or in the near future. An opportunity for an optician might be to sell protective and sports eyewear and a threat for a local shopkeeper might be a large supermarket coming into the area.

All available information on past performance of sales, market research, economic indicators and market shares should be studied and included where relevant.

The purpose of the SWOT analysis

- to match your strengths with opportunities in the market-place
- to eliminate some of your weaknesses and turn them into strengths
- to minimise some of the threats by using your strengths and turning them into opportunities.

For your company these activities will be your principle objectives for the coming year.

SWOT analysis

Internal   **External**

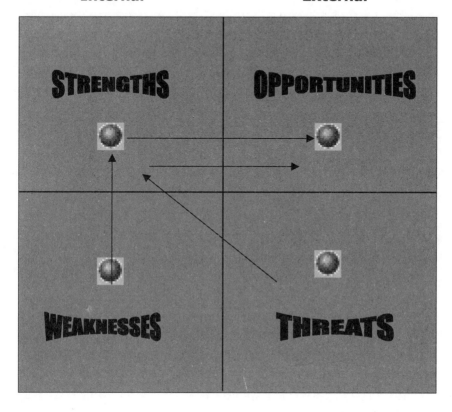

Another method of assessing the marketplace is to carry out what is often known as a PESTLE analysis or an audit of the external factors that affect the company's performance. PESTLE is a mnemonic for six different areas or topics which can be used to assess any marketplace.

The following areas or topics need to be considered and assessed for their input on your marketplace and business: **p**olitical, **e**conomic, **s**ocial, **t**echnological, **l**egal and **e**nvironmental.

Each area must be approached from the marketing perspective, i.e. customer implications, sales, buyer behaviour, competitive advantage, marketing implications etc. Of course the PESTLE method can be applied from a corporate viewpoint and is very useful for preparatory work on the business plan.

The *political* factors could include forthcoming legislation, possible European Union directives, preferences or election promises made by the government of the day.

The *economic* factors to be considered would include inflation, bank interest rates, levels of employment, employee incomes, taxation levels, consumer spending power, credit availability etc.

The *social* factors include people, cultural and societal issues — for example both parents working, working hours, cultural changes, social behaviour, use of free time, education of target market etc.

There are many *technological* factors to be assessed including new technologies in one's industry sector, use of the web and electronic communication and payment systems, advancements in computers and technology to improve products and services to customers, management information systems etc.

The *legal* situation is usually clear for each industry sector. Compliance with health and safety regulations, employment law, public liability etc. is necessary. Other legal issues include labelling, tracing products, local regulations and product safety, codes of practices and advertising restrictions.

A very important area for consideration from a marketing viewpoint is the *environmental* factors that affect the marketplace. Recycling toxic waste and caring for the environment are some of the key issues nowadays. As people are more concerned about ozone layers and their health in general, companies must also be seen to be active in these areas if they want to be attractive to broad consumer groups.

Objectives and goals

The above analysis is key to the next stage of the planning process, '*Where are we going?*' Every company should set itself objectives and goals so that it has a focus for the year ahead and also so that its performance can be measured and reviewed. The objectives are identified from the SWOT analysis, e.g. organise a sales training course, carry out market research on customer needs, identify targets outside your immediate catchment area. Goals are measurable targets which must be reached by the end of the year and usually focus on profit, growth, cash flow, new customers and new products. For example, increase profits by 10 per cent, sales to grow to ∈250,000, increase market share from 3 per cent to 5 per cent of the market, improve customer satisfaction from 67 per cent to 73 per cent etc.

Marketing strategies

You now need to identify '*How are we going to get there?*' For each of these objectives and goals you need to set out how they are going to be achieved. It is vital to choose the most suitable marketing strategies. There are several options outlined in the product/market matrix which may be appropriate to your business. There are four main marketing strategies suggested:

1. Increase market share.
2. New product development.
3. New target markets.
4. Diversification.

You can increase your market share by attracting your competitors' customers through effective advertising and increased sales efforts. Johnson & Johnson focused on baby products until they discovered that many mothers also used the products. Now a new range of hair and beauty products, PH 5.5, is aimed at the adult market, which for them was a new target market.

Every two years there seems to be a new product out from Pampers keeping them ahead of the competition.

Guinness launched draft Guinness in a bottle aimed at the pub/dance market. Product, price, place (distribution), promotional and people strategies will be needed to achieve the marketing and sales objectives.

The fourth option — new products to new markets (diversification) — is considered very risky and many companies have failed pursuing this strategy.

Product/market mix

	PRODUCT	
	Existing	**New**
MARKET — Existing	Increase Market Share	New Product Development
MARKET — New	New Target Market	New Products To New Markets

Source: H I Ansoff, *Corporate Strategy* (Middlesex, Penguin) 1968

It is vital for each marketing objective and goal that suitable marketing and customer care strategies are devised and a detailed action plan is set out with responsibility for its completion and a deadline date agreed. The example overleaf may make this approach clearer.

Marketing mix

For each of the strategies chosen, some parts of the marketing mix will be required. The marketing mix describes the *marketing tools* that are available, usually known as the Five Ps: product, price, place, promotion and people. The appropriate tool must be used to make sure that the strategy is implemented and the objective achieved. Within each part of the marketing mix a range of activities can be planned.

Philip Kotler devised the concept of the four Ps as a tool for implementing marketing activities (product, price, promotion and place, which is also described as distribution). Recently the staff and customer relations aspect of marketing has become so vital that a fifth P — people — is added to make the five Ps of marketing.

Action plans

At this stage most of the decisions have been made. The plan should document the specific actions for each objective/ strategy. Some staff person should be allocated responsibility for each action (who does what and by which date). This accountability is vital, especially at the end of year review of performance against the plan.

The non-financial aspects of the plan should be closely monitored (quarterly at least) to ensure that the competitive strategies are working. There may be a need to revise or amend your activities.

Marketing Objective No. 2: To increase our understanding of our customers needs and implement changes

Actions	Who	When
Marketing Strategy		
1. Carry out market research and customer satisfaction survey		
2.1.1 Brief research companies	MT/LL	Jan.
2.1.2 Select company	MT	Feb.
2.1.3 Survey and results	Research	March
2.1.4 Devise action plan	MT/LL/SOR	March
2.1.5 Communicate results to staff	MT	April
2.1.6 Plan repeat research	LL	Dec.
2.1.7 Organise competition among outlets	SOR	May
Marketing Strategy		
2. Retain staff and promote our customer orientation		
2.2.1 Select training company	LL	April
2.2.2 Devise customer care standards	Trainers	May
2.2.3 Train staff	Trainers	May
2.2.4 Devise customer charter	SOR	May
2.2.5 Charter/promise to customer	SOR	June
2.2.6 Change literature	SOR	June
2.2.7 In-store signs	LL	June
2.2.8 Direct mail to customers	MT	June

Budgets and controls

The plan is completed by allocating budgets for expenditure and sales income. Controls should be set up to ensure that performance against budget is monitored and does not get out of control without being noticed and actions are completed within the correct time frame.

Frequently there is a need to adjust budgets throughout the year to get a realistic view of performance to date. However, end of year reviews look at original budgets as well as adjustments in order to improve the planning process for next year.

DOCUMENTING THE PLAN

The full details should be documented in the marketing plan (see attached outline of a marketing plan) which is agreed by the relevant executives. There should be *collective ownership and responsibility*.

NEXT YEAR'S PLAN

Ideally there should be some indication of goals for year two and three in your plan. At the end of the year the plan should be reviewed and compared with the actual performance. Strategies and activities that did not work should be analysed in detail. This review will assist the planning process for next year's marketing plan.

MARKETING PLANS FOR PROFIT

If you do not have a marketing plan, with goals and targets or strategies to guide you, the chances of accomplishing an increase in profitability are at best haphazard. If, on the other hand, you do have a marketing plan with definite goals and action plans then you have a very reasonable expectation that the results will be achieved.

Below is a summary of the contents of a marketing plan.

Outline of marketing plan

1. Executive Summary

2. Background:
    - a. Company information
    - b. Products/services
    - c. Sales performance
    - d. Customers
    - e. Research results
    - f. Mission statement/vision
    - g. Past marketing activities

3. Marketplace Analysis:
    - a. PESTLE, (Political, Economic, Social, Technological, Legal, Environmental)
    - b. Competitors
    - c. Market sectors
    - d. Buyer behaviour

4. SWOT Analysis:
    - a. Strengths
    - b. Weaknesses
    - c. Opportunities
    - d. Threats

5. Marketing Objectives and Strategies

6. Marketing Mix
    - a. Product
    - b. Price
    - c. Distribution
    - d. Promotion
    - e. Customer Service

7. Action Plan

8. Budgets and Controls

Chapter Ten

Putting Marketing and Customer Care into Action

- Marketplace analysis is different for each company.

- Set clear marketing objectives and goals.

- Plan customer care policies and standards.

- Include customer care on agendas for management meetings.

- Devise clear action plans with responsibilities and timescales established.

Marketing plans can be quite different for each company. These plans need to be customised for your company and marketplace. There are, however, many common characteristics.

Below are some tables and grids which may be useful for setting out the topics and areas to be explored.

Marketing Plan

Mission statement

_____

_____

_____

_____

_____

SWOT analysis

Strengths	Opportunities
Weaknesses	Threats

Marketplace analysis (PESTLE)

External factors

Political

_____
_____
_____
_____
_____

Economic

_____
_____
_____
_____
_____

Social

_____
_____
_____
_____
_____

Technical

_____
_____
_____
_____
_____

Legal

_____
_____

_____
_____
_____

Environmental

_____
_____
_____
_____
_____

Competitor analysis

Key Competitors	Key Strengths
1.	
2.	
3.	

Customer analysis

Types of Customer	Share %
Industrial Segments	Share %
Products/Services	Share %

Source of new business

Source	Value

Marketing objectives

1. _____
2. _____
3. _____
4. _____
5. _____

Action plan

Marketing Objectives			
	Marketing Actions	Who	When
Marketing Strategy	_____		
	_____		
	_____		
Marketing Strategy	_____		
	_____		
	_____		

Customer care action plan

Theories and concepts on customer care are all very well, but how do you implement them? This part of the chapter sets out activities that need to be implemented if a company is serious about gaining a competitive advantage through superior customer care.

Firstly a reminder of the key customer care strategies that we already discussed.

1. Treat all customers as though they are lifetime customers — welcome the stranger!
2. Set up listening systems and measure customer satisfaction of the products and services provided.
3. Delight the customers whenever possible by providing something different and better than competitors.
4. Resolve complaints quickly and you can turn dissatisfied customers into delighted customers.

It is important to devise customer care policies for your company. Every staff member should be aware of them and practice them in their daily dealings with customers.

Moments of truth

Identify the 'moments of truth' on the cycle of service model below.

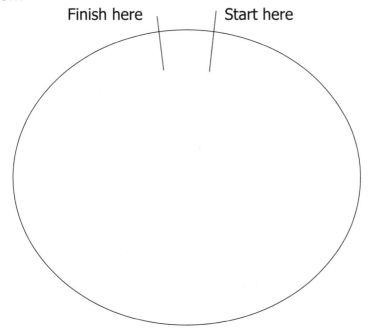

Finish here   Start here

Review each moment of truth and identify areas for improvement.

Unique Selling Points (USPs)

_____

_____

_____

_____

_____

Identify the unique selling points of your company, your products and services as well as customer care orientation. When finished examine your marketing and selling material and make sure that these USPs are included.

Features and benefits

Products and Services	
Features **(What it does)**	**Benefits** **(What's in it for the customer)**

Check if the text used in sales presentations and literature is focused on benefits rather than features. Remember, customers buy benefits not features.

Calculate the value of a lifetime customer

Describe a lifetime customer:

_____

_____

_____

_____

_____

Take an average customer and calculate the repeat purchase potential each week/month/year. Estimate the value of referrals (3/5) from a customer who is delighted and tells others who become customers.

For your customers — calculate their lifetime value

Year 1
Delighted customers spend ∈ ___ per week = ∈ ___ x 50 weeks
(sales/fees/income)   = ∈ ___ (yearly
spend)
Yearly spend ∈_____ x 10 years   = ∈ _____ = value of your
lifetime customer

Year 2
3 Customers are referred and they become delighted customers
3 X ∈_____ lifetime customers

In turn they will each recommend 3 more next year etc.

Identify key customer needs

_____

_____

_____

_____

_____

Customise for your industry and company. Be specific in terms of areas where you can measure their needs e.g. open from 8am to 8pm (not 'longer opening hours')

Customer Care Policy

The following grids are designed to assist in the implementation of customer care strategies and policies in your company. Some or all of the charts may be of use to you.

Set out in a statement the customer care policy of the company

_____

_____

_____

_____

_____

What is the company's policy on resolving complaints?

_____

_____

_____

_____

_____

Identify the different types of complaint that are received in your company

_____

_____

_____

_____

_____

What is the complaints procedure in your company?

_____

_____

_____

_____

_____

Listening systems

Identify the method and frequency by which the company will listen to and measure customer comments and opinions.
- Customer suggestion box?
- Market research?
- In-store signage?

Agenda for customer care meetings

Set out the areas of customer care that will be discussed at management meetings or specific customer care meetings.

_____

_____

_____

_____

_____

If appropriate, a cross-functional customer care committee should be set up and include staff who are interested in and whose performance is affected by customer care issues.

Action plan

Action	Who	When

An action plan is frequently needed to implement the many ideas identified by staff and customers. It is important to set dates and allocate responsibility to ensure the agreed actions are implemented.

TOP MANAGEMENT COMMITMENT

Superior standards of customer care will not just happen. The process needs to be managed and implemented. Commitment and leadership from senior management is absolutely necessary. It will be very frustrating for staff to prepare improvements to the level of customer care and find that senior management is apathetic or doesn't feel the need for these changes as they are not as committed to customer care when compared to their staff.

Customer care needs to be implemented with a passion and a commitment by all staff from the top down or superior customer care will not happen.

Bibliography

Suggestions for Further Reading

Ansoff, H I, *Corporate Strategy* (Middlesex: Penguin) 1968

Canning, Veronica, *Being Successful in Customer Care* (Dublin: Blackhall Publishing) 1999

Daffy, Chris, *Once a Customer, Always a Customer* (Dublin: Oak Tree Press) 1996

Kotler, Philip, *Marketing Management: Analysis, Planning and Control*, 10th edition (New Jersey: Prentice Hall) 1994

Levitt, Theodore, 'Marketing Myopia' *Harvard Business Review* (1960) July–August

Misner, Ivan R, *The World's Best Known Marketing Secret* (Texas: Bard Press) 1994

Quinn, Feargal, *Crowning the Customer* (Dublin: O'Brien Press) 1990

Raphael, Murray and Neil, *Up the Loyalty Ladder* (Dublin: O'Brien Press) 1995

Sewell, Carl and Paul B Brown, *The Golden Rules of Customer Care* (New York: Century Business) 1990

Index